REVELATION IN THE
FOURTH GOSPEL

—— GAIL R. O'DAY ——

REVELATION IN THE
FOURTH GOSPEL

Narrative Mode and Theological Claim

Fortress Press   Philadelphia

COPYRIGHT © 1986 BY FORTRESS PRESS

Library of Congress Cataloging-in-Publication Data

O'Day, Gail R., 1954–
   Revelation in the fourth Gospel.

   Bibliography: p.
   Includes index.
   1. Bible. N.T. John IV, 4–42—Criticism,
interpretation, etc.   2. Revelation—Biblical teaching.
I. Title.
BS2615.2.028   1986   226'.5066   86–45217
ISBN 0–8006–1933–1

2557B86   Printed in the United States of America   1–1933

For Jim

CONTENTS

PREFACE

This book addresses two contemporary scholarly conversations. The first conversation concerns the nature of revelation and in particular, the Bible as revelatory literature. The second conversation concerns the function of literary critical methodology in the interpretation of biblical texts. This book is an attempt to establish common ground between the two conversations. It suggests that the substance of revelation cannot be identified without careful attention to the literary mode of articulation.

Much of the initial work for this book was done for my dissertation at Emory University. At the dissertation stage, my work was aided by three scholars and teachers who were generous with their time and advice. Fred B. Craddock gave special insight at important points based on his interest in how texts communicate and how to communicate texts. Hendrikus W. Boers shared his expertise and knowledge of John 4, while at the same time allowing me the freedom to develop my own interpretation of this chapter. Finally, it was my privilege to have had William A. Beardslee as my dissertation advisor. He guided my dissertation with wisdom, perception, and care, and I will always be indebted to him.

My colleague at Eden Seminary, Walter Brueggemann, has helped me in critical and unnumbered ways as I have moved from being a graduate student to being a biblical scholar with my own voice. I am grateful for all that he has contributed to the writing of this book.

Finally, I would like to thank two people without whom this manuscript would not have seen completion. The first is John A. Hollar of Fortress Press, who worked carefully with my manuscript and from whose comments the manuscript has benefited greatly. The second is Donna Bass who, in the face of other demands on her time and work, carefully and attentively typed the final copy of the manuscript.

Gail R. O'Day
Advent, 1985

ABBREVIATIONS

au. trans.	author's translation
BAGD	W. Bauer, W. F. Arndt, F. W. Gingrich, and F. W. Danker, *A Greek-English Lexicon of the New Testament*
BDF	F. Blass, A. Debrunner, and R. W. Funk, *A Greek Grammar of the New Testament*
BJRL	*Bulletin of the John Rylands Library of Manchester*
BK	*Bibel und Kirche*
BVC	*Bible et vie chrétienne*
BZ	*Biblische Zeitschrift*
CBQ	*Catholic Biblical Quarterly*
ConBNT	Coniectanea biblica, New Testament
ET	English translation
ExpTim	*Expository Times*
FRLANT	Forschungen zur Religion und Literatur des Alten und Neuen Testament
HNT	Handbuch zum Neuen Testament
ICC	International Critical Commentary
Int	*Interpretation*
JBL	*Journal of Biblical Literature*
NovT	*Novum Testamentum*
NTD	Das Neue Testament Deutsch
NTS	*New Testament Studies*
RGG	*Religion in Geschichte und Gegenwart*

RSR	*Recherches de science religieuse*
SBLDS	SBL Dissertation Series
ThR	*Theologische Rundschau*
TS	*Theological Studies*
TZ	*Theologische Zeitschrift*
ZDPW	*Zeitschrift des deutschen Palastina-Vereins*
ZNW	*Zeitschrift für neutestamentliche Wissenschaft*
ZTK	*Zeitschrift für Theologie und Kirche*

INTRODUCTION

In our time, perhaps in every time, there is a yearning for revelation. We long for a word that will come to us from outside ourselves and create the possibility of life in a world that is closed. Only a revelation from God can break open our closed world and give this offer of life against death. We are convinced that God can and does offer such a life-giving and revealing word, but the problem of revelation for us is that we do not know how the revelatory word has access to us. Revelation is a problem among those who no longer believe a disclosure is possible. There is no access to revelation from such a starting point. Yet revelation is also a problem among those who are convinced that they can precisely identify how and when and where disclosure is located. That starting point, too, provides no access to a revelation that makes life possible in the face of death.

The community of faith responds to the yearning for revelation with the conviction that the biblical text is revelatory. But that conviction, too, has often been understood and articulated in ways that are unconvincing or that generate more problems. In reading the biblical text as revelatory, one makes a decision concerning how and where God is known. This book addresses the question of how it is possible to speak of the Bible as the revealed and revealing word of God.

The predominant approaches to the problem of revelation tend to define revelation through categories of dogma, doctrine, or philosophy.[1] The emphasis then falls on revelation understood as a noun. Yet revelation understood as a noun becomes static and fixed. When approaching the problem of revelation from a biblical perspective, another mode of understanding seems necessary. In order to answer questions of how and where God is known, it is more helpful to move from understanding revelation as a *noun* to understanding revelation as a *verb*. As a verb, revelation cannot become static but remains dynamic and generative.

If we think of revelation in terms of the verb *to reveal,* then we can ask, "How is God revealing?" "Where is God revealing?" and lastly, "What is God revealing?" If we ask first (and often, exclusively), "What is God revealing?" as is the tendency when revelation is understood as a fixed noun, then the mode and arena of God's presence become expendable as we focus our efforts on determining and classifying the subject of revelation. But as the theophanies of the burning bush (Exod. 3:1–22) and Sinai (Exod. 19:16–24) demonstrate, the mode and arena of God's presence are far from expendable.[2]

As for the problem of revelation for biblical studies, we need to ask how we can approach biblical texts in ways that affirm the mode and arena of God's revelation as well as the content, that include the object, subject, and mode of revelation. Literary critical analysis holds great promise in this regard, because its methodological presupposition is that the form and specific articulation of any given text must be taken with utmost seriousness and not regarded as incidental or extraneous. Literary critical methodology, then, provides access to questions of the mode and arena of God's presence that are not within the range of traditional historical-critical method.

The proposal of this book, offered through a detailed study of the Fourth Gospel, is that the substantive claims of revelation and the mode of disclosure are intrinsically related to one another. Every view of the Bible as revelation is unsatisfying if the substance of revelation is not tied to the mode of revelation through the very words of Scripture. The title and subtitle of this book indicate that I will approach the question of revelation by examining the interrelationship of narrative mode and theological claim in the Fourth Gospel. In particular, this book investigates how the Fourth Evangelist's use of one specific literary form, irony, provides him with the appropriate vehicle for his theology of revelation.

IRONY AND THE FOURTH GOSPEL

Irony is a widely recognized characteristic of Johannine style. Martin Luther, in his translation of the Fourth Gospel, made the following annotation about Pilate's question in John 18:38, "What is truth?": "It is irony. If you speak about truth, then you must be lost."[3] The standard commentaries on John all include entries for irony in their indices but make little or no effort to assess either the distinctiveness of Johannine irony or the theological significance of this literary technique. A few authors have attempted to deal with these questions, however, and their studies help to inform the context and perspective of our study of Johannine irony and revelation.

Studies of Johannine irony can be divided into two groups: those that give the most weight to literary questions in the study of irony in the Fourth Gospel and those that give the most weight to theological questions. In the first group, the most important studies are two recent books by R. Alan Culpepper (1983) and Paul Duke (1985).[4] Culpepper and Duke both have a balanced understanding of the dimensions of irony as a literary device and are able to build on this understanding in their analyses of the Fourth Gospel.[5]

Culpepper's treatment of irony in *Anatomy of the Fourth Gospel* is one section of a larger study of the literary structure of the Fourth Gospel. Culpepper's analysis focuses on Johannine ironic techniques and themes. He identifies six themes that are treated ironically in the Fourth Gospel: (1) rejection of Jesus, (2) origin of Jesus, (3) Jesus' identity, (4) Jesus' ministry, (5) Jesus' death, and (6) discipleship.[6]

In *Irony in the Fourth Gospel,* Duke provides a well-developed treatment of Johannine irony as a literary device. Duke's work complements that of Culpepper because both take similar approaches to irony in general and Johannine irony in particular. In his book Duke proceeds to analyze Johannine irony as a literary device under two rubrics: "local irony" (see chaps. 3 and 4 of his book) and "extended irony" (see chaps. 5 and 6). Local irony is that irony which occurs at a given point in the text, and it is analyzed by Duke in terms of speaker (e.g., Jesus, the disciples, the respondents), form (e.g., false assumption, unanswered question, misunderstanding), and theme (e.g., the sovereignty of Jesus, Jesus' death, discipleship). Duke's analysis of local irony leads him to the conclusion that in Johannine irony, *"form follows theme."*[7] Extended irony is irony that is developed throughout an episode or whole work. Duke analyzes extended irony first by surveying different types of situational irony (e.g., ironic characterization, ironic imagery), then by examining two specific scenes—the man born blind (John 9) and the trial before Pilate (John 18:28—19:16).

Duke addresses the question of the function of irony in his concluding chapter and arrives at a twofold function for Johannine irony. First, irony functions as part of the Johannine polemic against "the Jews." Second, and for Duke of primary importance, irony functions in support of the Johannine witness, offering a strong but indirect appeal to those who are open to its words.[8] The strength of Duke's work is that he concentrates on irony as a specific literary device and attempts to make precise what others generally and vaguely refer to as "characteristic Johannine irony." Yet his literary analysis leaves many of the larger theological questions open, for his assessment of the "why" of Johannine irony is more pragmatic than theological.

Culpepper and Duke both stress the role of Johannine irony in creating community, in drawing the reader into union with the evangelist. Duke calls the irony of the Fourth Gospel a "lure,"[9] and Culpepper compares it to "a net in which readers are caught and drawn to the evangelist's theology and faith."[10]

The most significant difference between these two studies and the analysis of Johannine irony undertaken in this book is the way in which ironic communication is characterized. Both Duke and Culpepper describe the wink, smile, or scowl that the evangelist uses to indicate the presence of irony. Culpepper writes that between reader and evangelist "a wink or smile creates a bond of secret communication,"[11] and perhaps of more significance for our study, Duke describes the relationship between the Johannine Jesus and irony in the following way, "The heavenly revealer of John's Gospel speaks irony too, but his eyebrows are raised and there is a trace of a smile upon his lips."[12] The connection between Johannine irony and the Johan-

4

nine theology of revelation is much more profound than this, however. The description of the Fourth Evangelist's (and Jesus') ironic stance as a wink or smile obscures the connection between the literary and theological dimensions of irony. Duke and Culpepper both give thorough and insightful analyses of irony as a literary device, but they leave untouched many of the larger theological issues.

Over a decade ago, George W. MacRae produced a study of Johannine irony that belongs to the second category mentioned above, studies which give the most weight to theological questions.[13] The question that guides MacRae's study is, "What does the Fourth Evangelist's use of the literary device of irony imply for our understanding of his theology?"[14] MacRae begins with the general description of irony offered by E. M. Good in his study of irony in the Old Testament (a "perception of incongruity" between appearance and reality).[15] MacRae further specifies the nature of Johannine irony as dramatic irony "in that it presumes upon the superior knowledge of the reader to recognize the perspective in which the Gospel's assertions are ironical."[16] In Greek tragedy, the irony arises because the author and spectator are aware of the distance between themselves and the events depicted on stage. MacRae notes, however, that this is not how ironic distance functions in John.

> But precisely where the distance of tragedy is meant to bring about catharsis without actual terror, in the Fourth Gospel this distance has the effect of involving the spectator in the challenge of faith. For the factor of distance in John is precisely the post-Easter perspective, the perspective of faith in Christ as the Logos vindicated by death and resurrection. It is this knowledge, which the Evangelist shares with the reader, which creates the ironical atmosphere that surrounds Jesus in his earthly career.[17]

By noting the particular interrelationship of distance and involvement in Johannine irony, MacRae indicates how John has taken a characteristic element of irony and accommodated it to his theological purposes.[18]

MacRae explicitly addresses the relation between irony and theology in the Fourth Gospel by considering John's "ironic vision." He observes that in John, irony "is not confined to the dramatic device but represents a whole literary (and quasi-philosophical) outlook.

5

. . . It is through this ironic vision that the contact with Johannine theology is made, for it is in irony that John expresses his own insight into the meaning of Christ for the world." MacRae goes so far as to say that in the Fourth Gospel, "theology *is* irony."[19]

> In a word, the heart of the Johannine theology is itself the irony of the Logos becoming flesh and dwelling among men, the revealing Word graciously announcing to men their own potential for eternal life in the self-giving act of love that is the return of the Father.[20]

MacRae pursues the study of irony in the Fourth Gospel primarily from the evangelist's perspective, namely, how his use of irony expresses his theological stance. It will be helpful to combine this approach with a study of irony from the reader's perspective, namely, how John's use of irony invites the reader to share his theology. Methodologically our study falls between that of MacRae and those of Duke and Culpepper. It will provide a more rigorous literary analysis than MacRae does, but it will put more emphasis on the integration of literary and theological dimensions than Duke and Culpepper do.

The Appropriateness of Irony for Fourth Gospel Study

These studies point to several reasons why irony is an appropriate category with which to study the Fourth Gospel. One reason, as the preceding quotation from MacRae indicates, is John's use of the Logos concept. As MacRae explicitly mentions, and others have noted without using the term irony, Logos itself is ironic.[21] We are presented with a literal meaning—a human being—and are asked simultaneously to accept it and to see in it the intended meaning—the divine. Rudolf Bultmann describes this relationship as a paradox, but his own portrait of the Logos is actually more ironical than paradoxical ("If a man wishes to see the *doxa* then it is on the *sarx* that he must concentrate his attention, without falling victim to appearances.")[22] The irony of the Logos is essential to the dynamics of revelation in John, because the source of conflicts and misunderstanding in the Gospel narrative is frequently the inability of those with whom Jesus speaks to comprehend both levels of Jesus' identity at once.

Another reason for irony's appropriateness indicated by these studies is that the Fourth Gospel, like all successful irony, depends on the audience sharing some knowledge with the author. A complete unanimity of thought and understanding is not required, because that is in part what John hopes to attain through his ironic technique, but some common context is presupposed—a shared frame of reference about Jesus and God. The post-Easter perspective supplies this common context. John's introduction of the Paraclete highlights the centrality of this perspective in the Fourth Gospel. John stresses two levels of comprehension, one before and one after the teaching of the Paraclete. Yet for John, one cannot simply define these two levels of comprehension chronologically. Instead, these two levels are intertwined in the Gospel. The Fourth Gospel narrative dramatizes these levels as overlapping one another, for example, in the disciples' remembrance and full understanding of Jesus' temple saying, achieved through the Paraclete (14:25), at 2:22.[23]

These two levels of comprehension point to another characteristic of the Fourth Gospel that links it with irony, its dualism. (Culpepper and Duke have drawn attention to the relationship between Johannine dualism and irony.)[24] The ironic statement is one in which two conflicting levels of meaning are contained within one verbal expression. This implies that

the ironist would tend not to think in terms of a singular absolute. Everything comes in more or less opposing pairs. For him, a belief achieves its reality, its life, its validity, only through conflict with its opposite. And the dualistic view of life is conveyed not only in the content of his statements, but most dramatically by the style itself, whose defining feature is that it at once offers two different meanings, the literal and the intended.[25]

The dualism of the Fourth Gospel—light/darkness, life/death—is so widely recognized in Johannine studies as to have become a commonplace. But this quality goes beyond these pairs of polar opposites, and many scholars have noted how a dualism pervades the style and structure of the gospel itself. Oscar Cullman has studied the function of "double-meaning" expressions in the Fourth Gospel. These expressions are words that communicate two meanings simultaneously, like *hupsoō,* for example, which means both "to lift up" and "to exalt" (cf. 3:14, 8:28, 12:32). Cullman interprets these "double-meaning" expressions through the lens of salvation history. The ambiguities in the double meanings are clarified when the events in Jesus' life are placed into their proper context in the entire history of salvation.[26] J. Louis Martyn, in an attempt to locate the historical setting of the Fourth Gospel, identifies another two-level structure. In his analysis of John 9, Martyn writes that the chapter is "presented as a formal drama, and allowed to mount its actors, so to speak, on a two-level stage so that each is actually a pair of actors playing *two parts simultaneously.*" Martyn attributes the two levels to the "dramatic interaction between the synagogue and the Johannine Church."[27] John simultaneously presents the events in Jesus' life and the events in the life of his community.

It is clear that scholars with diverse goals and methodologies have sensed how central stylistic and structural duality is to the Fourth Gospel, but until Duke and Culpepper, no explicit connection between this duality and Johannine irony had been made. Johannine irony provides the overarching category through which to view Johannine dualism. Yet Duke and Culpepper put too much emphasis on polar opposition in the dualities that they identify (e.g., "below" and "above") and not enough emphasis on the ways in which John presents these dualities as *simultaneously* operative in the Gospel. John does not present a simple either/or situation. Through his use of irony, the Fourth Evangelist asks the reader to see the real meaning *in* and *through* the expressed meaning, not as independent or removed from it (to use Bultmann's terms, the *doxa* [glory] must be seen *in* the *sarx* [flesh]).[28]

IRONY AND THE JOHANNINE THEOLOGY OF REVELATION

In looking specifically at the relationship between irony and the Johannine theology of revelation, two more areas of contact suggest themselves. First, Jesus' statements about his activities and function as revealer support the use of irony as a category with which to

interpret revelation in the Fourth Gospel. Just as every ironic statement requires an act of judgment on the reader's part to size up both
levels of meaning and to make the correct move from the literal to
the intended meaning,[29] Jesus as revealer presupposes the same dynamic of understanding:

> Jesus said, "For judgment I came into this world, that those who do
> not see may see, and that those who see may become blind." (John
> 9:39)

Jesus as revealer challenges customary concepts of perception. The
roles of those who see and do not see may be reversed.[30] Those who
encounter Jesus' revealing words will either become "blind" to them
and be unable to move beyond the literal level or will "receive sight"
and be able to make the necessary judgments and movement to
comprehend both levels of his statements. The responsibility for the
interpretation of Jesus' words is placed on each individual, which is
why Jesus is able to say that he comes both to judge and not to judge.
Jesus, through John, provides the keys to interpreting his words; the
reader must follow his lead in order to participate in the revelation.

Second, John provides the reader with an overt clue that he is
deliberately using veiled language to present Jesus as revealer. In
16:25 Jesus says, "These things I have said to you in figures (en
paroimiais); the hour is coming when I shall no longer speak to you in
figures (en paroimiais) but tell you plainly (parresiạ) about the Father."
The association of paroimia and irony was not unknown in John's
time, as Quintilian includes paroimia in his list of ironic methods (Inst.
8.6.57).[31] Similarly, Plutarch's ironic use of proverb (paroimia) is well
documented.[32] In John 16:25, however, paroimia does not refer to
isolated units of Jesus' teaching but to all of Jesus' teaching prior to
his glorification. The disciples' response in 16:29–30—"Ah, now you
are speaking plainly (en parresiạ), not in any figure (paroimia)! Now we
know that you know all things, and need no one to question you"
—shows that they are aware of the dynamic in Jesus' revelation
between direct and indirect expression. The full context of the verses
shows, however, that the disciples still do not completely understand
this dynamic, because Jesus chastises them for their surface confession of faith (16:32–33). The tension between speaking "in figures"

(en paroimiais) and "plainly" *(en parresiạ)* is identical to the tension that characterizes the two levels of meaning in irony and is essential to the Johannine dynamics of revelation.[33]

This book will investigate the ways in which the Fourth Evangelist uses irony in the Gospel narrative to create and recreate the dynamics of revelation. The many dialogues, discourses, and encounter scenes in the Fourth Gospel point to the importance the Fourth Evangelist puts on the communication process and the varied dynamics involved in the encounter with Jesus. Revelation is not static and fixed but dynamic and generative. One of the aims of this book is to demonstrate that the Fourth Gospel does not merely present a report of Jesus as revealer but allows the reader to experience the revelation for himself or herself.

In order to arrive at an understanding of the interface between *narrative mode* and *theological claim* in the study of revelation in the Fourth Gospel, it is necessary to be precise about both the mode and the claim. For that reason, before proceeding to an analysis of the Fourth Gospel text, it is important to give attention both to what irony is and how it functions and to the problem of revelation in the Fourth Gospel. Chapter 1, therefore, provides an examination of the essence and function of irony as a mode of communication. Chapter 2 provides a discussion of the different approaches to revelation that have impacted Fourth Gospel study. The heart of the book lies in chapter 3, which provides an analysis of what the interrelationship of narrative mode and theological claim tells us about revelation in the Fourth Gospel through a careful study of one Johannine text, John 4. Chapter 4 extends the conclusions reached from the study of John 4 to other parts of the Fourth Gospel.

1

THE ESSENCE AND FUNCTION OF IRONY

Irony is a difficult term to define, a difficulty which, we shall see as our discussion continues, is inherent in the very nature of irony and therefore unavoidable. We hear the word "irony" used frequently in everyday conversation, but often used so broadly as to include anything which strikes the speaker as dissonant, contradictory, or surprising.[1] If we bring only this fluid contemporary understanding and usage of irony to the Fourth Gospel, we will be unable to articulate with any precision the Fourth Evangelist's literary-theological method and accomplishment. For that reason we must begin with a careful analysis of the essence and function of irony.

This analysis of irony will follow two separate but often overlapping approaches: the historical, which focuses on the development of "irony", and the topical, which focuses on the function and operation of irony in literature. Irony was a widely recognized rhetorical device at the time of the Fourth Gospel, and an analysis of the origin and development of irony will provide us with a historical context for the study of Johannine irony, because it will indicate something of the scope of irony in John's time. As this historical analysis itself will show, however, the study of the development of irony only tells part of the story of its presence and function in texts, both ancient and modern. For this reason, it will also be helpful to pursue a topical analysis of irony that will focus on the questions involved in recognizing, reading, and interpreting irony. The integration of the histori-

11

cal and topical approaches provides the proper context for the study of Johannine irony and its role as revelatory language.

THE BACKGROUND OF "IRONY"

Aristophanes and Plato

The understanding of irony as a specific rhetorical device reflects a secondary development of the term *eirōneia.* In the earliest stages of its use, irony referred to a mode of behavior. Aristophanes and Plato, the first classical authors to use the term *eirōn* and its derivatives, use it to indicate mockery, slyness, and dissimulation.[2]

In Aristophanes the person who talks or acts *eirōnikōs* is someone who, under the pretense of harmlessness, is full of craftiness and guile.[3] In Plato the terms *eirōn* and *eirōneia* also have predominantly negative connotations, usually referring to Socrates' stance of feigned innocence and dissimulation. Socrates was depicted as someone who toyed with the words of his conversation partners[4] and who avoided answering direct questions.[5] Socrates, like Jesus of the Gospels, answered questions with questions.[6] The terms are not used positively by either Socrates or his associates to describe Socrates' method.

Yet the mere presence of the terms *eirōn* and *eirōneia* is not enough to indicate Aristophanes and Plato's conceptions of irony. Many of their works are themselves actualizations of this term, their sense of irony moving beyond the isolated (if not incidental) occurrences of the word "irony." Aristophanes communicates his sense of ironic mockery and dissimulation through the classic struggles in his comedies between the character with the wily traits of the *eirōn* (although rarely specifically so named) and the *alazōn,* the foolish braggart. *The Clouds* is the quintessential example of this Aristophanic technique, made doubly effective when Socrates, the traditional *eirōn,* is cast as the *alazōn.* Throughout Plato's dialogues we are able to see the actual workings of Socrates' ironic demeanor, even when the specific terms are not present. Although the words *eirōn* and *eirōneia* themselves have negative connotations, the dialogues show the positive effects of the Socratic method. It is this enactment of ironic behavior in the Platonic dialogues that helped to elevate *eirōneia* from a term of pure abuse to

12

one with slightly positive connotations.[7] One is already able to see in the works of Aristophanes and Plato the complexities involved in defining irony. The mere presence of the terms *eirōn* and *eirōneia* does not fully indicate the development and use of irony, in these cases as ironic behavior.

Aristotle and His Successors

The positive connotations of *eirōneia* implied by many of the Platonic dialogues are interpreted more explicitly, later on of course, in the *Nicomachean Ethics* of Aristotle. In this work Aristotle classifies *eirōneia* and *alazōneia* as understatement and exaggeration respectively and compares them both with the mean of truthfulness. Aristotle's taxonomical genius is evident in this classification. The pairing of these two qualities reflects the traditional pairings of the *eirōn* and *alazōn* as depicted by Aristophanes and other comic playwrights. Aristotle's definition of the *eirōn* is one who "disclaims or belittles the qualities he possesses." Those who employ *eirōneia* are nobler than the braggarts because they at least do not dissemble for their own advantage.

> Those who depreciate themselves by understatement are evidently more subtle in character. For, it seems, their speech is not motivated by profit, but by [the concern] to avoid bombast. They disclaim especially those qualities which are highly valued by others, as Socrates used to do. When they disclaim insignificant and obvious qualities, they are called "humbugs" and are more contemptible. Sometimes this is obvious boastfulness, as for example Spartan dress. In fact, both excess and exaggerated deficiency tend to be boastful. But people who make moderate use of self-depreciation and understate such of their own qualities as are not too noticeable and obvious strike one as more cultivated. It is the boastful man who is evidently the opposite of the truthful man, because he is inferior [to the self-depreciator.][8]

This description of *eirōneia* makes two important contributions to the development of irony. First, it identifies irony with understatement, an identification that is still made today. Second, and with far-reaching implications, Aristotle explicates and identifies positive aspects of *eirōneia* with the attitude and behavior of Socrates, thereby mitigating much of irony's offensiveness.

That the identification with Socrates was what gave irony its redemptive value can be seen most clearly by comparing Aristotle's attitude toward *eirōneia* in the *Nicomachean Ethics* with that in the *Rhetoric*. In the *Rhetoric*, where it is no longer a question of presenting the model of Socratic behavior, Aristotle judges irony much more harshly. In a discussion of fear, Aristotle lists among those enemies and rivals who should be feared "those who are mild, dissemblers *(eirōnes)*, and thorough rascals, for it is uncertain whether they are on the point of acting, so that one never knows whether they are far from it."[9] The *eirōn* is clearly someone who cannot be trusted. Similarly, irony can also give rise to anger—"And they are angry with those who employ irony when they themselves are in earnest; for irony shows contempt."[10] One seems far from the "cultivated" ironic behavior of the *Ethics*.

The *Rhetoric* does attribute one positive role to irony. Aristotle, quoting Gorgias, notes that it may sometimes be useful in debates "to confound the opponents' earnest with jest and their jests with earnest." As for the types of appropriate jests, "Irony is more liberal than buffoonery; for the first is employed on one's own account, the second on that of another."[11] This question of irony's appropriateness is important in later rhetoricians, especially Cicero.

The two threads in Aristotle's discussion of irony, the ethical and the rhetorical, are pursued separately by two of his followers. Anaximenes of Lampsacus, to whom *Aristotle's Rhetoric to Alexander* is attributed, pursued the rhetorical thread, and his use of the pseudonym Aristotle leaves no doubt that he wanted to locate his work within the Aristotelian tradition. His definition of irony was an important articulation of the rhetorical view of irony and is still the common dictionary definition of irony today: "Irony is saying something while pretending not to say it, or calling things by the opposite of their real names."[12]

The ethical thread can be seen in the Peripatetic philosopher Theophrastus, who begins his *Characters* with a portrait of the *eirōn*. Although Theophrastus' introduction to all thirty characters places the study within the Aristotelian school,[13] his portrait of the *eirōn* is more Aristophanic than Socratic or Aristotelian.[14]

Now dissembling *(eirōneia)* would seem, to define it generally, to be an affectation of the worse in words and deed; . . . If you are borrowing of your friends and put him (the *eirōn*) under contribution, he will tell you he is but a poor man; when he would sell you anything, no it is not for sale; when he would not, why then it is.[15]

Theophrastus' *eirōn* is a cowardly hypocrite, a caricature out of the same mold as the portrait of Socrates in *The Clouds.* The positive qualities of irony advocated by Aristotle are completely absent.

Cicero and Quintilian

The positive evaluation of irony reappears in Cicero, who incorporates aspects of both the ethical and rhetorical lines of Aristotle's thought in his discussion of irony. Cicero discusses two categories of irony in his works. The first is a straightforward rhetorical classification under the rubric "jests dependent upon language." An ironic jest is one in which the meanings of the words are inverted, when "you assert exactly the contradictory" of what you think.[16] Cicero, following Aristotle, divides jests into two classes, "the one coarse, rude, vicious, indecent; the other refined, polite, clever, witty," and categorizes the ironic jest as that which is refined and dignified.[17] Within this category of ironic jest, Cicero delineates a new form—"A jest very closely resembles this ironical type when something disgraceful is called by an honorable epithet. . . . "[18] This form of jest developed into a very popular ironic technique, commonly referred to as "blame-by-praise."[19]

Cicero's second category of irony is much more complex:

Irony too gives pleasure, when your words differ from your thoughts, not in the way of which I spoke earlier, when you assert exactly the contradictory . . . but when the whole tenor of your speech shows you to be solemnly jesting, what you think differing continuously from what you say.[20]

Irony is not just one particular manifestation of a rhetorical device but can color the entire content and tone of a speech, much as it does in Plato's dialogues.[21] Cicero locates this form of irony in the Socratic dialogues and, even more strongly than Aristotle, praises the use of irony on the basis of its use by Socrates.[22] The ethical and rhetorical come together in this evaluation of irony, for it is impossible to distinguish clearly between the pervasive irony of Socrates' speaking and his behavior.

In classifying this second category of irony, Cicero seems to acknowledge the complexity involved in analyzing irony that we noted above in the discussion of Aristophanes and Plato—*irony continually moves beyond classification by narrow definition.* Cicero's own works are further testimony to this complexity, because his actual use of irony in his writings, especially his correspondence, is much richer than his theory of irony.[23] The extent to which irony pervaded his work can be seen most clearly in the fact that almost all of Quintilian's examples of successful irony are drawn from Cicero's works.[24]

Quintilian, like Cicero, was interested in irony as a tool in argumentation. His purpose in writing the *Institutes of Oratory (Institutio Oratoria)* was "the education of the perfect orator,"[25] and it was in that context that he undertook his study of irony. Both following and citing Cicero, Quintilian advocates the use of irony as a way to render the judge "attentive to what we have to say."[26] In this context Quintilian defines irony as "the term which is applied to words which mean something other than they express."[27] Quintilian alternates between this more open definition of irony and that definition which equates irony with saying the opposite of what one thinks.

The heart of Quintilian's discussion of irony is found in Books 8 and 9 of the *Institutes.* The two categories of irony spelled out in Cicero are discussed under their traditional rhetorical designations—trope and figure. In Book 8 Quintilian defines a trope as "the artistic alteration of a word or phrase from its proper meaning to another,"[28] and in Book 9 he defines a figure as "the term employed when we give our language a conformation other than the obvious and ordinary,"[29] in other words, "a form of expression to which a new aspect is given by art."[30]

In his discussion of tropes, Quintilian notes that some tropes are employed to help out meaning and others to adorn style.[31] Irony belongs generally to this latter group[32] and is classified specifically as a type of allegory: irony is "that class of allegory in which the meaning is contrary to that suggested by the words."[33] Quintilian adds to previous discussions of irony as a trope by providing his audience with clues to the detection of irony in a speech.

> This is made evident to the understanding either by the delivery, the character of the speaker or the nature of the subject. For if any one of these three is out of keeping with the words, it at once becomes clear that the intention of the speaker is other than what he says. In the majority of tropes it is, however, important to bear in mind not merely what is said, but about whom it is said, since what is said may in another context be literally true.[34]

Although Quintilian's criteria for the detection of irony are limited because they are oriented to specific manifestations of irony in a speech, his observations nevertheless foreshadow three concerns that are central to modern studies of irony and that will be important in the analysis of Johannine irony. First, his emphasis on delivery, speaker, and subject reflects an integrated approach to identifying and interpreting irony, one in which internal and external factors play a role.[35] Second, Quintilian highlights the question of the speaker's ironic intention, and third, he draws attention to the importance of taking the context seriously, noting that any ironic statement could be literally true in another context.[36]

Quintilian's definition of irony as a figure in Book 9 is essentially the same as that offered by Cicero—the whole meaning and tone of a speech can be colored with irony. This effect of irony on meaning is the central difference between irony as a trope and irony as a figure.[37] In fact, the figurative use of irony can so influence meaning that one can actually speak of the impact of irony on a person's whole life. Quintilian compares all three types of irony in the following quotation:

> In the first place, the *trope* is franker in its meaning, and despite the fact that it implies something other than it says, makes no pretense about it. . . . But in the *figurative* form of irony the speaker disguises his entire meaning, the disguise being apparent rather than confessed. For in the *trope* the conflict is purely verbal, while in the *figure* the meaning, and sometimes the whole aspect of our case, conflicts with the language and the tone adopted; nay, a man's whole life may be colored with *irony*, as was the case with Socrates, who was called an *ironist* because

he assumed the role of an ignorant man lost in wonder at the wisdom of others. Thus, as continued *metaphor* develops into *allegory,* so a sustained series of tropes develops into this *figure.* [38]

In this passage Quintilian recognizes that irony is more than an ordinary rhetorical device, thereby touching "on this borderline where irony ceases to be instrumental and is sought as an end in itself."[39] The way for a more expansive interpretation of irony was set by this recognition. Most rhetoricians who followed Quintilian, however, did not pursue this aspect of his work (nor did Quintilian himself, since his primary concern was the place of irony in the education of the orator). Instead, they focused on the more pragmatic, limited uses of irony—saying the opposite of what is actually meant, blame-by-praise, and praise-by-blame.[40]

These observations by Quintilian are further indications of the interpretative flexibility involved, indeed required, in the study of irony. The definitional complexity noted throughout our discussion also receives explicit mention in Quintilian. In his introductory remarks on figures, Quintilian notes that many rhetoricians find it difficult to distinguish figure from trope in the study of irony.

> As regards irony, I shall show elsewhere how in some of its forms it is a trope, in others a figure. For I admit that the name is common to both and am aware of the complicated and minute discussions to which it has given rise.[41]

Although Quintilian, like Cicero, was primarily interested in the overt use of irony as a rhetorical device, both were forced to acknowledge that this view did not do justice to the known character and function of irony. The expansion of irony from a trope to a figure showed that irony was not purely verbal but could be involved, more covertly, with meaning and thought as well. But even this expansion did not adequately define irony, for as Cicero noted, the Platonic dialogues as a unit were characterized by irony.[42] Irony could therefore also be a quality of extended written works. The basic definition accepted by Cicero and Quintilian—to dissemble by saying the opposite of, or something other than, one means—only partially conveys the nature of irony. In order to capture and communicate the scope of irony, the field of observation must be expanded beyond the limits of oratory.[43]

THE EXPANSION OF "IRONY"

The rhetorical theory of Cicero and Quintilian dominated the use and discussion of irony for over fifteen centuries. It was not until the late seventeenth and early eighteenth centuries that irony began to move out of the purely rhetorical realm and into the realm of fiction and poetry. As the limited ironic techniques outlined by Quintilian were expanded into more comprehensive literary techniques by such writers as Jonathan Swift, Alexander Pope, Daniel Defoe, and Henry Fielding, critics began to recognize irony as an important literary mode and "for the first time defined the field of irony as the totality of an imaginative work of art."[44] This shift from irony as a rhetorical device to irony as a literary mode drew attention to a quality of irony which Cicero and others had only noticed in passing—that irony could shape extended written works.

This developing awareness of irony as a literary mode was given a new twist by irony theorists in Germany toward the beginning of the nineteenth century. These men, in particular the Schlegel brothers, Friedrich and August Wilhelm, and Karl Solger, not only analyzed the role of irony in extended written works, but also focused on the irony which they felt was inherent in the very act of artistic and literary creation.[45] Romantic irony, as this theory of irony came to be known, is characterized by a heightened self-awareness, which is reflected in the Romantic authors' consciousness of their relationship to their works. The relationship between author and work is seen as analogous to that between God and creation—the author was part of his or her work but could also look down on it from a detached position. This increased self-awareness brought with it an increased "recognition and acceptance both of the complexity and contradictoriness of the world and the obligation to come to terms with such a world."[46] Romantic irony highlights the incongruities of both the artist in relation to his or her art and human beings in relation to their world.

The impact of Romantic irony on subsequent studies of irony

cannot be overemphasized. First, it opened the way for conceptions of irony whose primary focus is not on irony in literature but on irony in life itself. Many contemporary categories of irony are derived from or overlap with Romantic irony—general irony, unstable irony, cosmic irony, metaphysical irony, irony of events. These modern derivatives, unlike the original Romantic irony, have in common the view that life and all its component parts are absurd. These radical forms of irony combine the individualism of the Romantic movement with a sense of the collapse of the reliable universe in which life (and language) take place.[47] Classical Socratic irony, the incongruity sensed between expression and meaning, is extended to its widest possible girth.

A second way in which Romantic irony exerted its influence, and the area of particular importance for our study of John, is the new slant that it gave to specifically literary approaches to irony. Not only was literature written after the advent of Romantic irony influenced by this movement,[48] but Romantic irony provided the impetus *to look back* to literary predecessors for examples of irony at work. The works of Cervantes and Shakespeare were hailed by many as embodying basic ironic methods and principles.[49] Of particular interest for our study and for all attempts to identify and analyze biblical irony is the work of Bishop Connop Thirlwall, who applied the new recognition and appreciation of irony to ancient texts, the plays of Sophocles.[50]

Thirlwall had close contacts with the ideas of the Romantic theorists—he translated the works of the German Romantic Ludwig Tieck —and the Romantic influence is readily apparent in his study. He introduces his discussion of Sophoclean irony with a more general discussion in which he notes three types of irony: (1) verbal irony, (2) dialectical irony (Plato, Blaise Pascal), and (3) practical or situational irony (irony not found in words but in the situation itself).[51] Thirlwall's analysis of dramatic irony begins with a thoroughly Romantic description of the dramatic poet, "The dramatic poet is the creator of a little world, in which he rules with absolute sway and may shape the destinies of the imaginary beings to whom he gives life and breath according to any plan that he may choose."[52] This created world gives the tragic poet the arena in which to express the interrelationship of life, history, and the "unseen hand" that guides their activity. The interplay of these factors "affords abundant room for the exhibition of tragic irony."[53]

Thirlwall then discusses his view of tragic irony in relation to the specific plays of Sophocles. In *Oedipus the King* he notes that the main theme of Sophocles' irony is "the contrast between the appearance of good and the reality of evil."[54] The irony of *Antigone* arises because Sophocles impartially presents and juxtaposes the sides of both good and evil.[55]

Thirlwall appears to have been the first person to discuss *explicitly* the notion of tragic irony and to associate this discussion with the ancient Greeks. In fact, the idea of tragic irony was so new that Thirlwall begins his essay by saying, "Some people may be a little surprised to see *irony* attributed to a tragic poet . . . ,"[56] a comment surprising to us today because we so readily make the connection between the Greek tragedies and irony. This aspect of Thirlwall's work is of particular importance for our interests. Thirlwall successfully applied new concepts to ancient texts without distorting the ancient texts. On the contrary, he highlighted essential characteristics of those texts. The Greeks themselves had no word for the kind of irony which Thirlwall identified, although Aristotle's description of *peripeteia* in the *Poetics* (1452a) contains some of its characteristics. Yet it is clear that the Greek tragedians had a sense of irony as both a literary device and a comprehensive literary vision. Thirlwall and others who further elaborated the concept of tragic irony do not read irony into the Greek texts but give a name to something that is already there. Thirlwall's analysis of Sophoclean irony confirms what we sensed in our discussion of Plato and Aristophanes—what the earliest writers explicitly said about *eirōneia* does not cover the full range of irony in antiquity. The study of Greek tragedy makes clear that it is legitimate and often necessary to inquire into the use of irony where the explicit term is not present, since the ancient use of the words *eirōn* and *eirōneia* had limited applications.[57]

Summary

This explanation of "irony" places specific ironies and texts in a larger context than that provided by the classical rhetoricians alone. It is now possible to see irony functioning both as a specific rhetorical device and as a more encompassing literary mode. In order to understand fully these two complementary dimensions of irony, however, we need to move beyond a historical analysis of irony and address ourselves to the specific task of identifying and reading irony. To do this we need to ask a new set of questions: how do we recognize and read irony, how is irony created, and what literary purpose does irony serve? It is to these and similar questions that we now turn.

THE OPERATION OF IRONY: FIELD OF OBSERVATION

As we begin a topical analysis of the operation of irony, it is important to specify our particular field of observation. As noted above, the field of observation refers to that area in which irony is noticed. We are not concerned with the more radical forms of irony but with that irony which presupposes both an artist and a medium and, in particular, with that irony which presupposes an author and a piece of literature. The traditional designation of this type of irony is verbal irony, which is adequate if one means by that "any irony deliberately created with words." It is inadequate, however, when it implies only those ironies created by specific literary devices. For example, in her analysis of *Tom Jones,* Eleanor Hutchens distinguishes between verbal and substantial irony. Verbal irony occurs when the language of a statement perpetrates the irony, substantial when the substance of the statement does.[58] This is an illegitimate distinction, however, destructive of the very nature of literary texts, because the substance of a statement is also part of its verbal quality. Any division made between the ironic content of a text and its ironic techniques will never arrive at an integrated interpretation of the text.[59]

In further distinction from the broad understanding and use of irony in much modern literature and criticism, we are also concerned only with those ironies that presuppose an act of interpretation in their creation. In other words, the author intends his or her irony to be seen through and understood, not to remain permanently absurd.[60] Wayne Booth calls this quality of irony its stability—the author expects the reader to move with him or her through the incongruities of the verbal irony and to arrive at a new, more coherent sense of the ironic statement.[61] Such ironies are also finite, because they presuppose a closed set of relationships, in contrast to general irony in which everything is relative.[62] The incongruities are a means to an end, not an end in themselves.

By focusing on those aspects of irony which are manifested and contained in a particular literary text, we are undertaking a rhetorical study, not in the classical sense with its restriction to oratory, but in the sense of trying to discover "the way irony works in uniting (or dividing) authors and readers."[63] Our primary concern is with the ways in which irony shapes communication between author and reader through the medium of the text.[64]

THE RECOGNITION OF IRONY

Irony and Other Figurative Language

In order to read irony, we must be able to recognize it. One of the first steps toward this recognition is distinguishing irony from other forms of figurative speech, particularly allegory and metaphor. The standard definition of irony, "saying one thing and meaning something else" or "saying something while pretending not to say it," really is nothing more than the etymological sense of allegory.[65] Quintilian's classification of irony as a form of allegory has been noted, but he was not alone in this practice. Many rhetoricians followed his lead.[66] This identification was appealing even to more modern interpreters of irony—"Irony could be called, in the proper sense of the word, an *allegory*, or even better, a *pseudologia*, because it thinks one thing and at the same time says something else."[67] Yet this identification blurs the fundamental distinction between irony and allegory. Booth makes the important observation that if the reader misses the second level of meaning in an allegory, he or she will still move in the general intended direction of the story—the literal and intended meanings do not conflict with one another.[68] That is not the case with irony, however. *There is always some kind of opposition between the two levels of meaning in irony—either contradiction, incongruity, or incompatibility.* [69] This tension gives irony its distinct character and makes reading and interpreting it more difficult than reading and interpreting allegory.

The similarities between metaphor and irony are also often noted.

23

Both adhere to that general pattern of "saying one thing and meaning another." Both "present two levels of meaning which the reader must entertain at once if he is to respond imaginatively to either of these forms of expression."[70] The difference between them again lies, as with allegory, in the element of opposition between the two levels of meaning. In metaphor the assimilation of one meaning into another is made smoothly, because metaphor points in the direction of its meaning. The transition to the principal subject *(tenor)* through the secondary subject *(vehicle)* is indicated openly in the construction of the metaphor itself.[71] In irony the transition is not as smooth—one level of meaning always conflicts with the other.[72]

One false distinction frequently made between metaphor and irony is that metaphor is a process of addition, whereas irony is essentially one of subtraction.[73] This distinction stems in part from the modern definition of irony, which implies that in order to understand irony, one merely has to substitute one meaning for another. But this is not how one reads irony—the intended meaning cannot simply be abstracted from the literal meaning, but the two must always be read in concert. The correct reading of irony involves a continual awareness of the "felt presence and felt incongruity of both meanings."[74] Irony is not "merely a matter of seeing a 'true' meaning below a 'false,' but of seeing a double exposure on one plate."[75] Irony involves as much addition as metaphor does, but this addition is fraught with tension and incongruity.

Another difficulty in recognizing irony is that one cannot say categorically that one form of speech is always ironical or that another one never is. Any form of speech (or literary genre) has ironic potential. Certain forms, for example, paradox, double entendre, understatement, exaggeration, have a higher probability of ironic use than others, but one cannot automatically assume that an author is being ironical merely on the basis of these forms. Irony may operate through these forms, "but is not to be confused with or defined by its rhetorical manifestations."[76]

The relationship between paradox and irony is a case in point. Paradox and irony are often used synonymously. For example, in the glossary to Cleanth Brooks and Robert Penn Warren's *Understanding*

Fiction, the entry for "paradox" reads, "See Irony."[77] The sole meaning given to paradox is as a form of verbal irony. This simple identification obscures the differences between paradox and irony and makes definitional clarity impossible. While it is true that paradox is one of the most common ironic devices, it can also be used without ironic overtones. Paradox is openly contrary to ordinary expectation. The contradiction does not, as with irony, lie in the relationship between two levels of meaning but is stated quite clearly in the literal meaning. John the Baptist's announcement of Jesus' coming in the Fourth Gospel is pure paradox: "He who comes after me ranks before me, for he was before me," openly contradicting normal expectations of the function of order and rank.[78] This contradiction is contained in the actual statement and not in a tension between two levels of meaning. One can, of course, create a context in which this paradoxical statement would become highly ironic, for example, as part of a Johannine polemic against the followers of John the Baptist, but the statement itself is not ironic.

Signals to Irony

If one cannot automatically assume that the use of a particular form indicates an ironic statement or text, then how can one recognize and interpret irony? The answer lies in the signals which the author himself or herself provides as pointers to ironic intention. Before analyzing some of these signals, two cautions must be given. First, signals to irony are often difficult to detect, because the essence of irony is to be indirect. A straightforward ironic statement would be a contradiction in terms. The ironist's challenge is to be clear without being evident, to say something without really saying it.[79] The author must therefore provide the reader with signals to the irony without shattering the tension between the two levels of meaning.[80]

The second caution is that the law of diminishing returns operates in ironic techniques.[81] In other words, the more frequently one writes ironically, the less effective the technique becomes in jarring the reader's expectations and in leading him or her to reexamine the literal meaning. This fact explains the observation made earlier, that any form of speech is potentially ironic. Therefore, any catalogue of signals to irony will always be only suggestive, never a definitive list. With these two cautions in mind, we will now analyze signals to the presence of irony in a text.

The most basic indication of irony in a text is the presence of "some form of perceptible contradiction, disparity, incongruity or anomaly."[82] This contradiction may be found in three separate areas, in the relationship between (1) text and context, (2) text and co-text, or (3) text and text (i.e., between one level or aspect of the particular text or passage under consideration and another).[83] To these three we turn, one by one.

First, context refers to the background out of which, in which, and for which the author writes. This context may vary "from a single fact to a whole sociocultural environment, from what is known to or felt by the addressor and addressee alone to what is universally accepted."[84] The specific signals that indicate a disparity between a text and its context vary accordingly, but several general principles apply. One signal is a conflict of beliefs between those which we assume the author to hold and those which he or she professes in the text under consideration (either in the author's own voice or in the voice of one of the characters). For example, we sense that Jonathan Swift is being ironical in *A Modest Proposal* because it is impossible to believe that he would seriously advocate child cannibalism. We also suspect irony when known historical facts are contradicted or historical probability stretched to the breaking point. In Samuel Johnson's dictionary, the definition of irony is illustrated with the saying, "Bolingbroke was a holy man." We can recognize this statement as ironical because it contradicts accepted fact. The reader may also suspect irony when there is a discrepancy between the text and accepted social standards, cultural norms, or moral values.[85]

Second, co-text refers to the specific literary context of the text, the context created by the author himself or herself. Booth points to the author's use of titles and epigraphs as possible signals of ironic intention.[86] Similarly, when an author interrupts the flow of a text with his or her own comments, as, for example, Henry Fielding does throughout *Tom Jones* or John does several times in the Fourth Gospel

26

(e.g., 11:49–52), one can often suspect that the passage before or after the interruption is intended ironically. D. H. Green has done the most systematic analysis of co-textual signals to irony, some of which include:

1. The possibility of suggesting irony by means of a parallelism between two scenes.
2. Passages that stand out by virtue of a heavy concentration of ironic remarks, so that the very concentration of irony constitutes an argument in itself when there is a measure of doubt about any one particular example and may tip the balance in favor of an ironic interpretation.
3. Passages in which a figure in the work uses irony and their correlation with passages in which, like such a figure, the poet or narrator can be seen employing the same technique.[87]

A few examples may help to illustrate and clarify these co-textual signals. A perusal of the detailed table of contents of *Tom Jones* indicates the innumerable ironies created by the juxtaposition of scenes. The presentation of Mr. Bennet, the unmercifully ironic father in *Pride and Prejudice,* is an excellent example of how a heavy concentration of ironic remarks provides an argument in itself for the presence of irony. The reader of *Pride and Prejudice* is constantly on notice to read for irony whenever Mr. Bennet speaks.[88] A Jane Austen novel also provides an illustration for the third signal to co-textual irony mentioned above. Henry Tilney, the male protagonist in *Northanger Abbey,* offers ironic commentary throughout the novel on the social conventions that make up the fabric of the world in which *Northanger Abbey* is set. He thus frequently assumes the same role and function played by the author-herself.[89] Henry Tilney's ironic commentary helps to interpret Jane Austen's commentary and Jane Austen's commentary helps to interpret Henry Tilney's ironic commentary.

Co-textual signals, then, can be classified into two general groups: (1) those which indicate the presence of irony through a disparity between the text and the literary context in which it is embedded and (2) those which indicate the presence of irony through a continuity with other passages in the same work in which similar language and oppositions occur. Signals to irony from both general groups are

27

found in the Fourth Gospel. The trial before Pilate (18:28—19:16) is an example of a scene in which the signals to irony are found in the disparity between the text and its literary context. The incongruity between the scenes with Pilate and Jesus and those with Pilate and the Jews (as well as the internal incongruities) indicate the presence of irony. The dialogue between the man born blind and his Pharisaic interrogators in John 9:24–34 is a good example of the second classification of co-textual signal. The heavy concentration of ironic remarks in the passage (e.g., 9:27, 28, 34) puts the reader on notice that an ironic interpretation of the scene is called for.[90]

The first two types of signals to irony we have discussed are intertextual: they arise from a disparity between the particular text under consideration and its context, in either a sociocultural or literary sense. The final group of signals to examine are intratextual. The intratextual signals to irony, those which indicate a disparity within different levels of the particular text itself, show the most resemblance to the analysis of irony in the rhetorical handbooks. Quintilian listed several ironic methods: sarcasm, urbane wit, contradiction, and proverbs.[91] The presence of such techniques remains a potential signal to the use of irony. Intratextual signals run the full gamut of literary and stylistic techniques. Some of the most important indicators are an abrupt change in style or tone, the use of words with double meanings and textual ambiguity, and the use of rhetorical questions, understatement, overstatement, parody, paradox, repetition, and metaphor.

None of these three classes of irony signals can adequately indicate the presence of irony by itself. Although Quintilian remarked that a disparity in any one of the factors that he listed—delivery, speaker, or subject—was a sure indication of ironic intention, one really needs the combined evidence of all three classes to recognize and interpret irony correctly. The signals provided by one class are enhanced and strengthened by those from the other two. The final confirmation of any one irony signal is always the integrated interpretation of the text itself. Or, as D. C. Muecke states,

> in any particular case of irony the irony marker can be confirmed as such only retrospectively, that is when one has understood the irony.

But in this the interpretation of irony is not different from interpretation in general.[92]

THE AUTHOR/AUDIENCE RELATIONSHIP

For irony to succeed, that is, for the signals to be detected and the irony to be interpreted and understood, the author must establish a relationship with the audience. The author and audience must share some knowledge and perceptions; if the audience does not have the knowledge necessary to work through the incongruities of the stated and intended meanings, no communication can occur. The relationship created between author and audience develops in two directions. It builds on a shared frame of reference out of which both author and audience operate, and it is also strengthened through the process of sharing ironies. Both parties to the irony—creator and recipient—must feel that they are "moving together in identical patterns."[93] Otherwise the irony will not work.

The relationship created between author and audience on the basis of shared knowledge is always stressed in the discussion of dramatic irony that has developed from the work of Thirlwall (see pp. 20–21). Indeed, the basic definition of dramatic irony centers around the audience's superior knowledge of events and characters in the play, derived from its role as spectator and from the information with which the playwright supplies it: "Dramatic irony, in brief, is the sense of contradiction felt by the spectators of a drama who see a character acting in ignorance of his own conditions."[94] Discussions of dramatic irony are often misleading, however, because this shared superior knowledge is not restricted to drama. All authors and audiences of irony, whether in narrative, poetry, or drama, hold some knowledge in common. Dramatic irony is only one manifestation of an operational principle essential to the communication of all irony.

Booth devotes considerable discussion to the communal nature of irony. He notes that talk about the victims of irony—those at whose expense the irony is created or who are excluded from it by lack of comprehension—is misleading because

> we need no extensive survey of ironic examples to discover that the building of amiable communities is often more important than the exclusion of naive victims. Often the predominant emotion when

reading stable ironies is that kind of joining, of finding and communing with kindred spirits.[95]

Interestingly, the example that Booth chooses to illustrate this point is from Mark 15:18, "Hail, King of the Jews." The opponents of Jesus offered this taunt as a satirical assault on Jesus and his followers, but its retelling in Mark gives it another irony.

> It is true that Mark may in part intend an irony against the original ironists, but surely his chief point is to build, through ironic pathos, a sense of brotherly cohesion among those who see the essential truth in his account of the man–God who, though *really* King of the Jews was reduced to this miserable mockery.[96]

This creation of community is a result of the performative aspects of irony. To speak of irony as performative means that irony does not just *say* something, it *does* something as well.[97] The indirectness of the ironic expression and the ironist's use of signals as pointers to the correct reading of the text require the reader to assume an essential part of the responsibility of making irony work. When the reader has finally recognized the irony and understood the text, his or her sense of involvement with the text is much greater than after reading a straightforward text. The judgments and decisions that the reader is asked to make, following the author's lead, create a strong bond between author, reader, and text that is as essential to the nature of irony as the creation of incongruities is. An ironic statement can never be successfully translated by a direct one because its performative aspects can never be translated;[98] the best one can arrive at is a paraphrase. Not only does irony show or tell a reader something, but it also involves the reader in the communication process, enabling him or her to participate in the text. What Arthur Sidgwick writes about the effect of irony on the reader's feelings applies equally to all forms of reader response and participation:

> the object of the highest expression is not to *represent* a fact or feeling to a passive percipient, to record it (so to speak) on a dynamometer of feeling, but to make him really *see,* by stimulating his imagination. If you wish to produce the effect, you cannot do it by mere word; you must get the hearer's imagination to help. And thus it often comes about that while the lower stages of feeling can be expressed, the

higher stages must be suggested. In the ascent the full truth will do; but the climax can only be reached by irony.[99]

IRONY AS A REVELATORY MODE

The irony with which we are concerned, verbal irony characterized by stability and finitude, is based "in a vision of truth."[100] The incongruities and tensions that draw the reader into the text are the means to draw him or her into participation in this vision, to make him or her "really *see.*" The author of such ironies does not create incongruities and oppositions in order to block meaning and comprehension but to intensify meaning and comprehension. In a comparison between pure deceit and irony, Vladimir Jankélévitch writes, "It is quite another thing if one deceives *while* helping or deceives *in order to* help, if one hides or misleads *while* guiding or hides *in order* to guide and reveal . . . ."[101]

Despite its apparent attempts to conceal meaning, *irony is a mode of revelatory language.* It reveals by asking the reader to make judgments and decisions about the relative value of stated and intended meanings, drawing the reader into its vision of truth, so that when the reader finally understands, he or she becomes a member of the community that shares that vision, constituted by those who have also followed the author's lead. Booth goes so far as to speak of "a community of believers" created through irony.[102] Drawing on Jankélévitch one could say irony conceals in order to reveal, hides in order finally to make visible. Such a mode of revelatory language cannot be reduced to propositions or abstractions but must be embraced in the fullness of its literary form.

We have now seen evidence of irony as both an explicit and implicit phenomenon, as a rhetorical device and a wide-ranging literary mode in ancient texts, and this provides an important context for our analysis of Johannine irony. We have also observed several factors involved in creating, recognizing, and reading irony that will aid us in identifying Johannine irony and in clarifying its use as a mode of revelatory language.

This understanding of irony as a mode of revelatory language is suggestive for our study of revelation in the Fourth Gospel. Rather than looking for the locus of revelation behind or in front of the literary text, the operation of irony as revelatory language suggests that the locus of revelation lies *in* the text itself. In the following chapters we will explore the possibility that the Fourth Evangelist found the perfect vehicle for his theology of revelation in irony. Through his use of irony as a revelatory language, John's *mode* of presentation renders the *object* of that presentation: the literary form in which Jesus is presented as revealer in John is inseparable from the Johannine theology of revelation.

2

REVELATION IN THE FOURTH GOSPEL

In the beginning was the Word, and the Word was with God, and the Word was God. He was in the beginning with God; all things were made through him, and without him was not anything made that was made. In him was life, and the life was the light of men. The light shines in the darkness, and the darkness has not overcome it.

There was a man sent from God, whose name was John. He came for testimony, to bear witness to the light, that all might believe through him. He was not the light, but came to bear witness to the light.

The true light that enlightens every man was coming into the world. He was in the world, and the world was made through him, yet the world knew him not. He came to his own home, and his own people received him not. But to all who received him, who believed in his name, he gave power to become children of God; who were born, not of blood nor of the will of the flesh nor of the will of man, but of God.

And the Word became flesh and dwelt among us, full of grace and truth; we have beheld his glory, glory as of the only Son from the Father. (John bore witness to him, and cried, "This was he of whom I said, 'He who comes after me ranks before me, for he was before me.' ") And from his fulness have we all received, grace upon grace. For the law was given through Moses; grace and truth came through Jesus Christ. (John 1:1–17)

No one has ever seen God; the only Son, who is in the bosom of the Father, he has made him known. (John 1:18)

The Fourth Gospel opens in John 1:1–18 with a hymnic prologue. John 1:18 occurs at a pivotal point in the Gospel of John.[1] This verse

33

functions as the transition from the prologue to the main body of the Gospel.[2] In the move from the prologue to the Gospel proper, the Fourth Gospel moves from a programmatic statement about the *logos,* the Word, to the concrete narrative embodiment and demonstration in the Gospel narrative of how that word is manifested and functions. John 1:18 provides the key to understanding this move from the hymnic statement of the opening verses to the narrative embodiment which begins in 1:19 by pointing to the purpose of the incarnation: to make God known.

How is God made known in the Fourth Gospel? Determining the ways in which the Johannine Jesus makes God known, or to use more traditional theological language, determining the nature of revelation in the Fourth Gospel, is one of the most basic questions in Fourth Gospel study. With the transitional verse of 1:18, the Fourth Evangelist signals us that this question is not a concern externally imposed upon this Gospel, but one intrinsic to its composition and function. The different answers scholars pose to this question reflect the varied presuppositions about where the locus of revelation lies. Is the locus primarily in the words of the text, in the message of the text, in the events behind the text, in the person behind the text, or in the proclamation in front of the text?

David Kelsey has shown quite clearly how the decisions one makes about the mode in which God is "present among the faithful" influence the ways one uses and construes Scripture.[3] In his seven case studies of twentieth-century Protestant theologians, Kelsey identifies three rubrics through which to construe the mode of God's presence. Each of these modes occasions a particular use of scripture:

1. The *ideational mode,* in which God is understood to be present through the content of Scripture, its doctrine and concepts (Warfield, Bartsch, Wright).
2. The *mode of concrete actuality,* in which God is understood to be rendered present completely and dynamically through Scripture (Barth, Thornton).
3. The *mode of ideal possibility,* in which God is understood to be present in and through existential events called forth by Scripture (Bultmann, Tillich).[4]

34

What becomes clear in Kelsey's study is that one's approach to and appropriation of Scripture is governed by one's understanding of revelation and one's answer to the question, "How is God known?"

The connections signalled by Kelsey have particular relevance for Fourth Gospel scholarship, because, as John 1:18 indicates, the mode of God's presence in the world is an essential concern of the Fourth Evangelist. The Fourth Evangelist states quite boldly that it is in Jesus that God is known, but that claim raises as many questions as it answers. The Fourth Gospel thus makes it impossible for its readers to avoid the question of the nature of revelation, and indeed, Fourth Gospel scholarship is a mirror reflecting the widely ranging views of revelation.

APPROACHES TO REVELATION IN THE FOURTH GOSPEL

Content

The special role accorded by John to Jesus' revelation of God has long been recognized by Johannine scholarship. In traditional nineteenth- and early twentieth-century liberal biblical scholarship, Jesus' revelation was approached from the perspective of its *content* and was analyzed in two general directions concerning what Jesus' revelation communicates (1) about God's nature and (2) about God's salvific and redemptive plan.

When the focus is on the content of Jesus' revelation of God, revelation is primarily understood as something that communicates *about,* and Jesus' revelation can therefore be understood and appropriated as a series of propositions and concepts. When this content is examined for what it reveals about God's nature, Jesus' revelation is translated into conceptual language that speaks of God's exemplary righteousness and love.[5] God's love is made known both through God's sending of Jesus and through the love of Jesus himself. The importance of this revelation of God's love lies in the moral example that it sets for the believer's life. Bernhard Weiss provides a classic statement of this view of revelation:

> [Christ] presents his own humbly ministering love . . . , His self-sacrificing love, . . . to be a pattern to us. Here also . . . the revelation

of God given in the exhibition of Himself is determinative for our moral life.[6]

The locus of revelation is thus seen to lie in the lesson that can be appropriated from the text. This understanding of revelation, characteristic of mainline German biblical scholarship at the turn of the century, is still present in contemporary scholarship of the Fourth Gospel.[7]

The content of Jesus' revelation can also be analyzed in terms of what it communicates about God's plan of salvation. From this perspective, Jesus' revelation is understood as part of the continuum of God's historical revelation of the divine plan of salvation. This plan of salvation began and was enacted in the Old Testament and reaches its consummation in Jesus. The Johannine Jesus brings God's righteousness and holiness, which had already been revealed in the Old Testament, fully into view.[8] The Fourth Evangelist is then understood as one who is

> convinced that the historical life of Jesus is the *centre* of the whole saving process of God, as well as being the centre of all God's revelation. . . . But the important thing for the evangelist is that God's self-communication, his saving activity, has its mid-point in the historical life of the man Jesus of Nazareth. . . . All revelation, all God's acting, is disclosed from this mid-point.[9]

The locus of revelation is thus seen to lie in the unbroken horizontal line of God's presence and plan in history to which the text bears witness.

These interpretations of Jesus' revelation of God in the Fourth Gospel, which focus on the content of that revelation, are characterized by two central points: (1) the revelation in Jesus is exclusively identified and analyzed on the basis of the Judeo-Christian experience of God; and (2) the revelation in Jesus is understood as providing us with a moral example to appropriate and follow. These two points, although based on presuppositions central to much of biblical scholarship, have been increasingly viewed by many scholars as inadequate categories with which to approach the text of the Fourth Gospel.

Comparative

One alternative approach was the comparative studies approach first offered by the history-of-religions school of New Testament interpretation.[10] This approach moved outside of the confines of the Judeo-Christian religious experience and sought to analyze the Bible as one among many expressions of the religious environment of the Mediterranean world. Parallels to New Testament expressions and thought forms were sought in Hellenistic mystery religions, Gnosticism, and other religious movements. The impact of this approach on Johannine scholarship and on the particular question of the nature of revelation in John cannot be overestimated.

In contrast to the approach to Jesus' revelation in John that focuses on content, the history-of-religions approach focuses more on the figure of Jesus as revealer and attempts to understand Jesus as the revealer/redeemer figure in the context of revealer/redeemer figures from contemporary philosophies and religions. The discovery and publication of major texts from different Mediterranean religions provide impetus and data for the comparative approach. The accessibility of major Mandaean documents, the Dead Sea scrolls, and the Coptic Gnostic documents of Nag Hammadi has stimulated research into what the Johannine figure of Jesus as revealer shares with other cultural representations.[11]

Careful comparative study of the *logos* and the redeemer myth as shared experiences and expressions of the Mediterranean world was particularly important in shaping the history-of-religions understanding of revelation in the Fourth Gospel.[12] The most enduring contribution to the question of the nature of revelation in John has come from comparing the Johannine Jesus with the redeemer figure in Gnostic redeemer myths.[13] The comparison with the Gnostic myth enabled scholars, led by Walter Bauer and Rudolf Bultmann, to understand the Johannine Jesus as belonging to the pattern of "the one sent from God," the preexistent essence of God who is sent into the world, who preaches with the power and words of the God who sent him, and who is in permanent unity with this God. Bultmann, for example, identifies twenty-eight points of contact between John and this basic Gnostic redeemer myth.[14]

In the history-of-religions approach to revelation in the Fourth Gospel, the dominant interpretive criteria are what Jesus as revealer and the nature of revelation in John share with other cultural expressions of divine revelation. The specificity of the revealer figure and the particularity of the content of the revelation are de-emphasized. The focus is on what holds true across cultural lines, not what is distinctly Johannine. *The locus of revelation is thus seen to lie in the mythical paradigms that are common to various cultural occurrences.*

The comparative approach views revelation from the perspective of common mythical paradigms instead of from the perspective of a specific historically delimited revelation. When the move is made away from the particularity of the biblical text to more general revelatory paradigms, the locus of revelation has shifted significantly. This initial move away from particularity allows another move to be made, to ask what is the essence of revelation behind or within the paradigm. It is not mere coincidence that the existential understanding of revelation in the Fourth Gospel has its roots in the history-of-religions methodology.

Existential

When revelation is interpreted existentially, it is understood neither as objective content nor shared paradigms but as the subjective truth about human existence that it evokes.[15] The mythical paradigms are important because they provide inroads into the language of the Fourth Gospel, but one must push beyond these paradigms to ask what view of authentic human existence is made possible by the Gospel and its language. The most articulate and influential spokesman of the existential approach to revelation was Rudolf Bultmann.

Bultmann was not content to view the mythic paradigms of the Fourth Gospel as a primitive explanation of the world but instead understood them as an expression of how each person views himself or herself in the world and felt that the Fourth Evangelist used such myths in order to call human existence into question.[16] Bultmann's provocative statements on revelation remain the catalyst for all discussions of Johannine revelation and have played a decisive role in determining the categories through which Johannine revelation continues to be approached. It is therefore important to examine the existential approach to the question of revelation in detail.

Bultmann is led to the existential analysis of Johannine revelation through his understanding of the function of the person of Jesus as revealer. He starts with the Johannine presentation of the incarnation. The Fourth Evangelist adapts the cosmic and mythological language used in Gnosticism to describe the earthly presence of the revealer, but moves beyond this language to convey his understanding of Jesus' incarnation. In Gnostic myths, the coming of the revealer is an act of condescension, the revealer's appearance signifying only that the revealer is now visible. In the Fourth Gospel, however, the incarnation is essential to the nature of revelation, because divine revelation confronts humanity in a specific human being. The incarnation is thus a paradox, because the glory *(doxa)* is to be seen in the flesh *(sarx)* and nowhere else.[17] The human flesh does not merely accompany the glory, nor is it an expendable vehicle for the glory (both views of Gnostic redeemer myths), but it is in the flesh of the incarnation alone that the glory is visible. Jesus' presence is therefore simultaneously offense and revelation, because as a mere human being he claims to speak for God.

What transpires in the human encounter with the paradoxical presence of Jesus as offense and revealer is central to Bultmann's existential analysis of the Fourth Gospel. Jesus' offense is intensified since he cannot and must not validate his claims before the world—his presence must be sufficient proof of his revelation of the divine.[18] But, if Jesus must not substantiate his claims, what is the content of his revelation? The answer to this question underlines the distance between the first approach to revelation we examined, that which focuses on content, and the existential approach. In the existential approach, as articulated here by Bultmann, the answer to the question regarding the content of Jesus' revelation is clear—Jesus' revelation has no content. Jesus does not communicate anything objectifiable (teachings, formulae, rites), as if he were only an expendable vehicle for the transference of information and knowledge. Instead, Jesus' paradoxical presence evokes decision and demands response.[19] The decision for faith through which one is saved occurs in the encounter with Jesus and in overcoming the tension between Jesus as offense and Jesus as revealer.

It is therefore not the content of what Jesus says or does, but the fact that an encounter with the divine occurs that is at the core of revelation in John. This important understanding of Johannine revelation is provocatively expressed in one of Bultmann's most well-known and debated statements, a precise articulation of his existential approach to revelation:

> Thus it turns out in the end that Jesus as the revealer of God *reveals nothing but that he is the Revealer.* And that amounts to saying that it is he for whom the world is waiting, he who brings in his own person that for which all the longing of man yearns: life and truth as the reality out of which man can exist. . . . But how is he that and how does he bring it? In no other way than that he is it and says that he brings it —he, a man with his human word, which, without legitimation, demands faith. John, that is, in his Gospel presents only the fact *(das Dass)* of the Revelation without describing its content *(ihr Was).* [20]

The contrast between fact *(Dass)* and content *(Was)* is pivotal to the existential understanding of revelation.

Bultmann thus understands Jesus' role as salvific revealer in terms of the light that the encounter with him sheds on the nature of each individual's existence. In the encounter with Jesus, the meaning of each person's existence is called into question, and the decision one makes in the face of this encounter reveals what authentic human existence is. Because there is no content to Jesus' revelation, God can only be known in the act of human decision. Such an understanding is central to the existentialist hermeneutic. No objectifiable information can be abstracted from the encounter with Jesus, no patently reassuring christological or theological teaching. All knowledge of God comes through Jesus with his stark demand for a response in faith.

The existential approach to revelation contrasts sharply with the other approaches to revelation we have examined. We have already seen that, in the existential approach, revelation is not understood in terms of propositions and concepts. Revelation is not a communication *about* anything. Similarly, just as revelation cannot be objectified into propositions, it also cannot be understood in terms of what it communicates about God's plan of salvation. Revelation cannot be assimilated into the traditional modes of linear history.[21] Bultmann consolidates all of salvation history into the one decisive event of Jesus' coming as revealer. There is no progressive unfolding of Jesus' revelation, because the *"Dass"* of revelation is punctiliar, not linear.

No series of events can be strung together to demonstrate God's progressive revelation in history, because revelation occurs in each moment of eschatological decision and only in that moment.

The contrast with the comparative approach to revelation is also clear. In the comparative approach, we noted that the locus of revelation lies in the common mythic paradigms and the world created by those paradigms. The existential approach moves beyond those common paradigms and establishes a new context for their use and interpretation. The Fourth Evangelist adapted the common redeemer myth but stripped it of its cosmological, mythological, and mystical dimensions. This reworking of the myth, or demythologizing, to use Bultmann's term,[22] left the Fourth Evangelist with only the bare fact *(Dass)* of revelation. This bare fact is not empty, however, but is the heart of revelation, because it is the encounter with the bare fact that calls human existence to decision and accountability.

In the existential approach to revelation in the Fourth Gospel, the focus is on the encounter with Jesus and the moment of decision evoked by Jesus' paradoxical presence as revealer. The revelation experience is neither repeatable through historical reminiscences about the "life of Jesus," nor through the recital of universal ideas or paradigms about Jesus, but can be recreated only when the word of Jesus, the fact *(das Dass)* of Jesus, is proclaimed by the Christian community. Whether one encounters Jesus in his specific historical moment or in the proclamation, the revelation is "in every case a personal moment in a personal history."[23] *The locus of revelation is thus seen to lie in the new understanding of human existence that emerges from the subjective encounter with Jesus.*

The existential approach to revelation, with its emphasis on God's presence in the moment of human decision, focuses on the evocative function of the biblical text. Scripture, and in our particular case, the Fourth Gospel, is not understood as objective language about God but as the vehicle through which the subjective experience of God becomes possible. God is therefore known in *existential event,* and this knowledge of God can never be translated into a definitive, fixed statement. This bold stance of the existential approach has triggered much response, particularly among scholars who disagree with its

understanding of the locus of revelation. The most influential response to the existential approach to revelation is the dogmatic approach.

Dogmatic

The dogmatic approach has close ties with the first approach to
revelation we examined, that which focuses on content. The dogmatic approach moves beyond the content approach, however, in
that it is developed in a broader context and proposes a different
locus of revelation. The broader context in which the dogmatic approach to revelation develops and operates can be seen in its engagement in explicit dialogue with the existential approach. The location
of revelation in the bare fact *(Dass)* of Jesus' presence as revealer is
challenged by a renewed insistence on the *Was* of Jesus as revealer.

The work of Ernst Käsemann is the most carefully articulated
presentation of the dogmatic approach to revelation in the Fourth
Gospel.[24] Käsemann critiques the existential reduction of the Johannine language to mere event. The Johannine language about preexist-
ence and the unity of the Father and Son occupy a pivotal position
in Käsemann's approach to the Fourth Gospel. The Fourth Evangelist
intentionally uses mythological language to establish an exclusive
relation between Father and Son. This relationship is essential to
Jesus' revelation because this unity is what makes it possible for the
Son to make God known. Any interpretation, in particular the existential interpretation, that attempts to modernize John's mythological language of unity fails to grasp his message.[25]

The language about the Father and Son cannot be stripped away
or regarded as secondary, because this language is the beginning of
dogmatic reflection on the nature and identity of Christ. The striking
characteristic of the Johannine proclamation is that it contains one
message that is rigidly and dogmatically repeated—the unity of the
Father with the Son. Through this repetition, "the exclusiveness of
Jesus as the revealer receives its foundation and safeguard."[26] This
dogmatic reflection on Jesus' identity forms the only object of faith
for the Fourth Evangelist and the only access to Jesus' revelation:

> Nowhere else in the New Testament is the faith described with such
> force, repetition, and dogmatic rigidity. Faith means one thing only; to

know who Jesus is. . . . John does not present us with a model of a Christianity without dogma. John's peculiarity is that he knows only one single dogma, the christological dogma of the unity of Jesus with the Father. Therefore one should not play off the kerygma against the dogma.[27]

Knowledge of Jesus and his revelation can only be established on the basis of dogma and verified through the working out of that dogma in the discipleship of the Church, not on the basis of subjective personal experience and personal decision.[28]

The Fourth Evangelist has deliberately presented Jesus' revelation in the categories of dogma. One cannot separate the fact of revelation from what is being revealed because the Johannine proclamation is inherently and intentionally dogmatic. Revelation can only be understood through the christological witness of the Fourth Gospel that is formulated in dogmatic categories. There is no access to Jesus' revelation independent of dogmatic reflection on who he is in relation to the Father.[29] *The locus of revelation is thus seen to lie in dogmatic formulations about the nature of Jesus.*

THE "HOW" OF REVELATION

This overview of four different approaches to revelation in the Fourth Gospel shows the variety of answers that can be given to the question, "How is God known?" and shows the link between the answer to that question and the interpretive framework through which one views the Gospel of John.

1. In the first approach, which answers that God is known in the *content* of Scripture, the Fourth Gospel is a source for lessons and examples about Jesus and God.

2. In the comparative approach to revelation, which answers that God is known through *mythical paradigms* contained in Scripture, the Fourth Gospel is an articulation of shared mythical language and paradigms.

3. In the existential approach, which answers that God is known in the *existential moment of personal decision* called forth by Scripture, the Fourth Gospel is the vehicle that facilitates the subjective experience of God.

4. Finally, in the dogmatic approach, which answers that God is

known in *dogmatic reflection* on the identity of Jesus, the Fourth Gospel is an articulation of christological dogma.

Here then are four different answers to the question, "How is God known?" and four different approaches to the Fourth Gospel. But how do these four approaches stand in relationship to what should be our control, the text of the Fourth Gospel itself? Do these views of revelation complement or conflict with the Fourth Evangelist's view? Do the presuppositions of these views lead us closer to or draw us farther away from the Johannine theology of revelation?

What seems to be missing in all these approaches to the Fourth Gospel is an understanding of the Johannine theology of revelation that takes seriously the Gospel narrative itself. In the views that focus on content and dogma as the locus of revelation the text is secondary to the propositions and abstractions that can be mined from it. In the comparative approach, what is particular to the Fourth Gospel narrative is secondary to what it holds in common with other cultural expressions. In the existential approach, the particularities of the text are secondary to the truths about human existence they call forth. But the Fourth Evangelist did not write a textbook, a theological treatise, a collection of paradigms, or a philosophical essay. He wrote a gospel, and we will never approach the Fourth Evangelist's answer to the question, "How is God known?" until we take the mode of articulation of the text seriously.

The secondary position assigned to the Fourth Gospel text in answering questions about the nature of revelation can be seen most acutely in the *Dass/Was* distinction, which is at the heart of the existential approach and which still establishes the parameters for most discussions of revelation in John.[30] The form the *Dass/Was* debate takes—whether revelation lies in the bare fact of Jesus as revealer or in the content of his revelation—allows almost no middle ground, middle ground that should be occupied by the Fourth Gospel text. From the *Dass* side, the particular form of the proclamation, the words of the text in and of themselves are insignificant, because as objective language, "every fixed form of words" becomes dogma.[31] The implications are that the particular text is not decisive in communicating revelation; any other form of textual expression could be equivalent (a similar presupposition is held by the comparative approach to revelation).

From the *Was* side, emphasis is placed upon the content of revelation (be it moral example, salvation history, or christological dogma), but little serious thought is given to the way in which that content is presented in the Fourth Gospel and what effect that presentation has on the content itself. On the whole, the emphasis on revelatory content reduces the Fourth Gospel narrative to formalized theological abstractions, which, as with the existential emphasis, ignores the particularity of the Johannine language and the interrelatedness of form and content in the Gospel narrative.

In reducing the revelation experience in the Fourth Gospel to either *Dass* or *Was,* in focusing strictly on revelatory content, revelatory paradigm, revelatory encounter, revelatory dogma, the total impact of the revelatory narrative of the Fourth Gospel is lost. In these different readings of revelation and the Fourth Gospel, the dynamics and interplay of the Fourth Gospel text itself as part of the revelation experience are virtually ignored. But such readings are not true to the text of the Fourth Gospel. The Johannine dynamic of revelation cannot be conveyed by the categories of event or content, kerygma or dogma. Revelation is not static in the Fourth Gospel and therefore cannot be understood independently of the Fourth Gospel narrative. Without full attention to the revelatory dynamic of the Fourth Gospel text, we are not in the world of the Fourth Evangelist.

The Fourth Evangelist presents his readers with a wide variety of intricate portraits of the encounter with Jesus and his revelation, none of which can be easily subsumed under the rubrics we have examined thus far. For example, John 1:19–51 narrates the call of the disciples and their immediate decision for Jesus, proclaimed with a broad array of christological titles. In the cleansing of the temple episode which follows in John 2, however, the disciples make no similarly immediate decision but can only arrive at full understanding later (2:22). Jesus' dialogue with the Samaritan woman (chap. 4), the progressive dawning of faith in the man born blind (chap. 9), and Thomas' reluctant acceptance of the resurrected Lord (chap. 20) are all different examples of the Johannine dynamic of revelation.

The Fourth Evangelist shapes and communicates revelation

through the particular literary characteristics of the Johannine narrative. In order to arrive at a more integrated understanding of revelation in the Fourth Gospel, we need to approach the question of revelation with categories that reflect the gospel's interplay of *narrative mode* and *theological claim*. The *Wie,* the "how" of revelation is one such category. The "how" of revelation is the narrative mode through which the Fourth Evangelist presents Jesus as revealer and communicates his theology of revelation. If we approach revelation in the Fourth Gospel from the perspective of the "how" of revelation, we may begin to discover the Johannine answer to the question, "How is God known?"

THE "HOW" OF REVELATION IN
THE FOURTH GOSPEL

The seemingly enigmatic quality of Johannine language has provided a beginning point for many literary studies of how Jesus functions as revealer in John. Attempts to decipher this language range from understanding the distinctive traits of Johannine revelatory language under the general rubric "parable,"[32] to classifying particular examples of the Johannine technique of misunderstanding under the specific form critical category of "riddle."[33] Alan Culpepper has done the most thorough study of the distinctiveness of Johannine literary style and technique to date, but he has done so in a general way without particular attention to the question of revelation.[34]

In order for literary studies to make a contribution to the discussion of revelation in the Fourth Gospel, however, questions of language, style, and technique must be asked in a consistently theological context.[35] Literary studies must also address the question, "How is God known?" The most explicit and helpful investigation of the relationship between Johannine revelatory language and the Johannine understanding of revelation is the work of Wayne Meeks.[36] Meeks has precisely articulated why the "how" of revelation is important. The focus of Meeks' literary analysis is Jesus' dialogue with Nicodemus in John 3. He focuses in particular on the ascent/descent motif that is articulated in John 3:13: "No one has ascended into heaven but he who has descended from heaven, the Son of Man."

This motif, which at first glance seems to provide warrants for Jesus' revelation,[37] actually points to a more complex set of relationships. Meeks' careful analysis of this text leads him to conclude that the language and speech forms in John 3 create a "virtual *parody* of a revelation discourse." Instead of clarifying Jesus' revelation, the language emphasizes Jesus' strangeness and incomprehensibility.[38] The reader of the dialogue feels sympathy for Nicodemus because in reading the dialogue, she or he has an experience similar to that of Nicodemus. The reader will either reject Jesus and his puzzling words, or will stick with them until the "progressive reiteration of themes . . . brings a degree of clarity." The reader's experience is thus "grounded in the stylistic structure of the document."[39]

At this point in his analysis of Johannine language, Meeks makes an observation that is pivotal to understanding the Johannine dynamics of revelation and that has gone unnoticed in virtually every previous discussion. Meeks observes that "the book functions for its readers in precisely the same way that the epiphany of its hero functions within its narratives and dialogues."[40] Meeks' observation reflects awareness of the interplay between *narrative mode* and *theological claim* to which we have been pointing. Any study of Johannine revelation that ignores the form, style, and mode of Johannine revelatory language will always miss the mark. The mode of revelation is not incidental but essential to the Johannine theology of revelation.

Literary analysis of the particularities of the Johannine text must therefore be integral to any discussion of revelation in the Fourth Gospel. When approached in this way, the Fourth Gospel is allowed room to have its say in its own language. Literary critical study of biblical texts, at present a growing trend in biblical scholarship, is not an externally imposed discipline when it is done with attention to the integration of the literary and the theological. Such methodology actually presents us with a way of reclaiming biblical texts and biblical faith. The presupposition of this approach to the Fourth Gospel is that form and content cannot be separated in discussions of revelation. *The locus of revelation is thus seen to lie in the biblical text and in the world created by the words of that text.* [41] We cannot answer the question, "How is God made known in the Fourth Gospel?" apart from a discussion of *how* Johannine language creates and communicates the revelation experience. The "how" of revelation must be taken seriously as an integrated literary and theological category.

We have spoken thus far in general terms about the "how" of revelation in the Fourth Gospel. Identifying the "how" as a more comprehensive category to apply to the Fourth Gospel text is the first step in understanding the Johannine revelatory dynamics. The second step is to identify the specific characteristics of this "how" in the Fourth Gospel. The discussion of irony in chapter 1 has provided us with the tools to look at Johannine irony as a mode of revelatory language. I propose to study the Fourth Evangelist's use of irony to create his portrait of Jesus as revealer and to recreate the revelation experience for his readers so as to demonstrate the specific "how" of revelation in the Fourth Gospel. An analysis of Johannine irony will provide access to the locus of revelation in the Fourth Gospel by underscoring the interrelationship of the literary and theological dimensions of revelation, the interplay of narrative mode and theological claim.

We shall proceed to use John 4:4–42 as a test case for examining the relationship of irony to the Johannine theology of revelation. This chapter in the Fourth Gospel depicts Jesus as revealer in three different contexts—in an encounter with an individual (the Samaritan woman) and with two groups (the disciples and the Samaritan villagers)—and therefore offers a multifaceted portrait with which to work. The dialogues of John 4 provide the reader with the opportunity to become involved in the verbal interplay between the characters but also allow him or her the distance and freedom to observe what is being enacted. The combination of direct and indirect communication which this chapter employs, highlighted by its use of irony, is central to the Johannine dynamic of revelation. John 4:4–42 is an important example of the relationship between the Fourth Evangelist's narrative mode, in particular his use of irony and his theology of revelation. A careful analysis of this chapter will thus enable us to move closer to the "how" of revelation in the Fourth Gospel.

3

REVELATION IN CONTEXT
(JOHN 4:4–42)

INTRODUCTION TO THE TEXT

Any casual reader of John 4:4–42 cannot help but notice that the chapter contains two seemingly distinct dialogues: one between Jesus and a Samaritan woman and one between Jesus and his disciples. The disciples are not present in the scene with the Samaritan woman, nor is the woman present during Jesus' conversation with the disciples. This apparent disjunction of scenes, coupled with other textual and thematic incongruities and inconsistencies, has led many scholars to question the textual integrity of this episode.[1]

Any seam in the text, for example vv. 8 and 27, is often viewed as an indication of later additions by the evangelist as he adapts the source material into a larger framework. These later additions are seen as secondary, with "only incidental ties to the story proper."[2] Robert Fortna, for instance, contends that when the secondary additions to the original story are removed (vv. 10–15, 20–24, 31–38), "a coherent story, with only slight Johannine retouching, remains."[3] While the story postulated by such source theories may be coherent, it is not the story that the Fourth Gospel finally presents to us. John 4:4–42 cannot be reduced to the story of Jesus trying to obtain a drink of water from a woman at the well, but it is the story of Jesus in conversation with the woman *and* with his disciples, and his conversation moves from well water to living water to true worship to the eschatological harvest. Whether or not the different scenes were once separate stories is a moot point in the analysis of the narrative of John 4, because the Fourth Evangelist has carefully molded them together into one story. Instead of viewing vv. 8 and 27 as clumsy seams that reflect the evangelist's attempts to attach one story to another, these verses should be viewed as signs of this author's careful crafting as he intentionally interweaves two complementary dialogues into a complex narrative with one beginning, middle, and end. As our interpretation of John 4 progresses, we shall demonstrate that all the sections of this chapter are intimately interrelated—each section leading to what follows or building from what has preceded.

It is therefore my working assumption that John 4:4–42 is an intentional literary unity, a composition that can and should be examined and interpreted in its final form. Whatever the composition history of the text may have been, it is obvious that the final product has been carefully planned, and it is with this final form that we begin to analyze John 4. This is not to deny the complexities of the text nor the author's possible use of sources in its composition but is instead to acknowledge that these complexities are part of the literary character of the text and must be interpreted as constitutive of its meaning. The meaning and interpretation of the text are not to be derived from its prehistory, but from its final form.[4]

Another factor that argues against reading some sections of John 4 as primary and others as secondary additions is the recognition of the thematic unity that draws the episodes together into a whole. There is a growing consensus that the central concern of John 4:4–42 is the question of Jesus' identity and that one way of interpreting the chapter is to see it as a portrait of Jesus' self-revelation. Many scholars have drawn attention to Jesus' self-revelation in John 4:4–42, to the series of key words and titles applied to Jesus, with its crescendo from Jesus as a Jew to Jesus as the savior of the world.[5] Such analyses of John 4 correctly emphasize the fact that John has carefully constructed this episode in order to highlight Jesus' self-revelation.

Yet if Rudolf Bultmann has overemphasized the *Dass* of Jesus' revelation, particularly as John presents it to us in John 4:4–42, much of the recent christological analysis of this scene has focused too stringently on the *Was*—that Jesus reveals himself as the Messiah

(4:26), that he is the savior of the world (4:42). This emphasis on *what* Jesus reveals is inadequate as a means of dealing with Jesus' self-revelation, because inseparable from the *what,* and of at least equal importance, is the factor of *how* Jesus reveals himself.[6]

The notice drawn to the dynamic self-revelation of Jesus through the titles touches upon the *how* of the revelation, but the ultimate focus of such studies remains on the titles and what they say about Jesus. The revelation of Jesus in John 4 is much more than that, and it is only by capturing the *how* in addition to the *Was* and *Dass* that we can comprehend all the dimensions of Jesus' self-revelation.

As indicated earlier, I contend that irony provides access to the *how* of revelation in John. The goal of my exegesis of John 4:4–42 is to demonstrate that this is so. I shall do this by a careful analysis of the Samaria narrative, focusing on its literary dynamics and examining how John's use of irony enables the reader to participate in the revelation experience. My aim is not merely to identify those instances in John 4:4–42 in which the Fourth Evangelist employs ironic techniques. Rather, I want to show how these techniques are used by the evangelist to develop his portrait of Jesus as revealer and to communicate his theology of revelation. First, we turn to a general outline for the Samaria scene, then proceed by following in detail the movement of the dialogues and narrative.

THE NARRATIVE FRAMEWORK

When one begins to dissect John 4:4–42, the Fourth Evangelist's careful interweaving of the different sections of the story becomes clear. A quick overview of the text establishes vv. 4–6 as the introduction, 7–26 as Jesus' dialogue with the Samaritan woman, 27–38 as Jesus' dialogue with the disciples, and 39–42 as the conclusion. A careful review of the narrative, however, reveals that it cannot be so quickly and crisply divided into distinct, self-contained sections.

The precise boundaries of the introduction to the Samaria narrative are to some extent problematic. Some scholars begin their analysis of the Samaria narrative with 4:1, others with 4:4 or 5.[7] The rationale for reading 4:1–4 as a unit is that together these verses establish the itinerary for Jesus' journey: from Judea to Galilee through Samaria. Verses 1–2 provide the reasons for this journey, the controversy over

Jesus' baptismal activity, and v. 3 records the journey's beginning. If we read the narrative carefully, however, we notice that v. 4 functions more as an interruption of the central journey than as part of its original itinerary. It takes us away from a concern with Judea and Galilee and draws our attention to Samaria. That this is a diversion, albeit a pivotal one, is shown by v. 43: "After the two days he departed to Galilee." After his two-day stay in Samaria, Jesus resumes his original journey.

Another factor that argues against reading John 4:1–3 as part of the introduction to the Samaria narrative is that, although these verses do provide the context for Jesus' journey, they also function as a conclusion to the preceding section (particularly 3:22–30) with its final testimony of John the Baptist. The primary function of these verses is thus to bring to completion the role of John the Baptist by focusing attention on the successful activity of Jesus and his disciples, and thereby turn the narrative focus from John the Baptist to Jesus. John 4:1–3 is a transitional section in the entire Gospel narrative, not an introduction to the specific events recounted in the Samaria episode.[8]

If we read v. 4 with vv. 5 and 6, however, there is no similar ambiguity about the narrative function of these verses. They are clearly the introduction to the Samaria narrative—v. 4 provides the specific reason for Jesus' presence in Samaria (Jesus *had* to travel through there), and vv. 5–6 furnish specific details about the location in Samaria that set the stage for Jesus' encounters there. The narrative receives its decisive starting point with these verses.

John 4:7 signals the beginning of Jesus' dialogue with the woman, for here the woman arrives at the well and Jesus first speaks, but the woman's response is not recorded nor the real interchange begun until after the evangelist reports the departure of the disciples. As noted above, the comment about the disciples in v. 8 has been seen by many as an intrusion by the evangelist into an independent pre-Johannine story. Although at first sight v. 8 may seem to interrupt the flow of Jesus' dialogue with the Samaritan woman, its effect on the total narrative is not intrusive at all. Rather, this verse informs the reader that the actions of the Samaritan woman and the disciples are never completely independent of one another. At this juncture, the narrated arrival of one character is balanced by the narrated departure of the other.[9] The relationship between vv. 7 and 8 reflects the relationship between the two larger dialogues as a whole, although only one dialogue at a time occupies center stage— the off-stage area is never just empty space. John has carefully positioned pointers in the narrative—of which v. 8 is just one example —that enable the reader to move from one stage to another, from one set of characters to another.[10]

The Samaritan woman's response to Jesus is recorded in v. 9, and Jesus' dialogue with her continues through v. 26. This dialogue can be subdivided into two sections: vv. 7–15 and 16–26. Each of these subsections begins with a request/command by Jesus (indicated by the imperative)—v. 7 "give me a drink" *(dos moi pein);* v. 16 "go, call your husband" *(hupage phōneson ton andra).* We shall return to the interplay within and between these subsections below.

Verses 25 and 26 bring Jesus' actual conversation with the woman to a close—v. 25 is the last word spoken directly by the woman to Jesus and v. 26 is the last word spoken directly by Jesus to her. The dialogue is formally brought to its conclusion, however, by the return of the disciples. As he did at the beginning of the dialogue, John explicitly narrates the movements of the characters, the return of the disciples in v. 27 and the departure of the woman in v. 28. The woman departs from center stage, Jesus and his disciples now occupying the well area, but she does not disappear immediately from sight. Instead John allows the reader to follow the woman off-stage for a minute, into the village from which the disciples have just arrived, and provides us with her interpretation of the scene that has just ended. The temporal reference in v. 31 ("meanwhile") indicates that vv. 28–30 are to be perceived as background activity to the central activity of the narrative. Verses 27–30 thus represent a highly developed transition scene that has its own important role in the narrative. It is a "narrative hinge" that serves both to end the first dialogue and to provide a context out of which the second dialogue can operate.

Set against the background of the Samaritan woman's activity in the village, the dialogue proper between Jesus and his disciples begins, as did the first dialogue, with a request/command. In v. 32 the disciples say to Jesus, "Rabbi, eat" *(phage)*. The conversation with the disciples continues through v. 38. Like the first dialogue, its completion is marked by the return of the other set of characters. The Samaritan woman does not return alone but is accompanied by others from her town who have come to believe in Jesus through her word (vv. 39 and 40).

The arrival of the Samaritan townspeople begins the conclusion of the narrative. Like the preceding two dialogues, this exchange begins with a request/command, although in this case the request is reported as indirect speech—the Samaritans ask Jesus to stay with them. Jesus complies with their request, and for the first time since the beginning of the narrative, he moves from the well. What had been off-stage, the Samaritan village, now comes to center stage as Jesus moves from the well to the village.[11]

These observations lead us to the following outline of John 4:4–42:

    I. vv. 4–6. Introduction: the setting of the narrative
   II. vv. 7–26. First dialogue: Jesus and the woman
      A. vv. 7–15. "Give me a drink"
      B. vv. 16–26. "Go, call your husband"
  III. vv. 27–30. Transition scene
  IV. vv. 31–38. Second dialogue: Jesus and the disciples
   V. vv. 39–42. Conclusion: Jesus and the Samaritans

This analysis of the narrative framework supports the comments made at the beginning of the chapter, that John 4:4–42 is a consciously composed literary unit. It is not a primary narrative with secondary accretions but one coherent whole.

The discussion of the narrative framework of John 4:4–42 has provided a brief overview of the scene's movement and development. We shall build on this outline below when we analyze the individual scenes. Before moving on to this detailed analysis, a few preliminary observations can be made that will contribute to an understanding of the dynamics of the narrative.

First, it is important to notice one of the ways in which John involves the reader in the text. He draws the reader from one narrative focus to another so that the reader is not given the opportunity to rest comfortably in one place; one is kept slightly off balance. An example of this is in the transition scene of vv. 27–30, when the story moves from the well to the village and back to the well. One cannot simply observe this narrative. One must move with it.

Similarly, as we have noted, John carefully juxtaposes and balances one scene with another, (see e.g., vv. 7 and 8, vv. 27 and 28, the placement of imperatives in the dialogues). A comparison of one set of characters with another, of one dialogue with another, is unavoidable. If we recall what was said in chapter one about co-textual irony (irony that arises from a contradiction or disparity between the text and its literary context), we can obtain an early indication of one of John's narrative techniques.

The Analysis of the Narrative

(4) He had to pass through Samaria. (5) So he came to a city of Samaria, called Sychar, near the field that Jacob gave to his son Joseph. (6) Jacob's well was there, and so Jesus, wearied as he was with his journey, sat down beside the well. It was about the sixth hour. (John 4:4–6)

This text begins with a surprising amount of information about the external features of the site of the events.[12] The setting of the narrative is important and cannot be overlooked when interpreting John 4:4–42. The Fourth Evangelist has taken great pains to describe the scene in detail, and as the narrative progresses we are constantly reminded of this locale.

The text opens with the notice that it was necessary *(edei)* for Jesus to pass through Samaria. Scholars are fairly evenly divided on whether or not this *edei* implies theological or geographical necessity. It is quite possible to read the verb purely on the level of the story line—Jesus, on his way from Judea to Galilee, felt obliged to take the shortest route, a route which took him through Samaria.[13] Yet if we examine the ways in which *dei* is used elsewhere in the Gospel (e.g., 3:14, 30; 9:4), we find that John almost always uses it with the sense of theological necessity. Is that a correct reading here?[14] As is often the case in interpretation, the answer cannot be given until the complete text has been read.

What is important to notice at this juncture is that the very beginning of this narrative invites the possibility of two levels of thought: does the necessity arise from the demands of the particular journey

55

or from the demands of God? The correct question is probably not one of either/or but of both/and: is the reader to understand that both mundane *and* divine necessity are operative here? We shall return to this specific question, as well as to the importance of seeing both/and instead of either/or, as our analysis of the narrative unfolds.

Verses 5 and 6 provide much of the raw material for the rest of the Samaria narrative. Verse 5 gives the precise location of the scene, but the geographical detail itself is not what is important. What is important is the religious, particularly patriarchal, terminology in which this geography is couched. Sychar receives its narrative significance because it is "near the field which Jacob gave to his son Joseph," in which was located Jacob's well.[15] Several important images that will be central to the further development of the narrative are introduced in these verses—the idea of giving, Jacob, Jacob as father ("to his son Joseph"), and the well. What appears as a purely descriptive statement will take on new meaning in the context of the total narrative.

The introduction ends with Jesus' arrival at the well. The description of this arrival establishes the conditions for his request for water in v. 7: Jesus was tired from his journey, and he arrived at the well in the heat of the day ("about the sixth hour").[16]

It is clear from these opening verses that the setting of this episode in Samaria is not incidental to the story line but will play an integral part in it. Although it is doubtful that the site at Jacob's well was a Samaritan shrine,[17] there is no question that in vv. 5 and 6 the Fourth Evangelist has described the scene in such a way as to point to central Samaritan religious traditions.[18] The function of this setting and these traditions will become clearer as we observe the interplay between Jesus and the Samaritans, but it is not too early to note that this Samaritan context sets the entire text in an ironic framework: 4:42 will underscore the point that Jesus has success among the Samaritans but not among his own people. While this irony is not restricted to a theology of revelation, it is related, because it draws attention to the question of who does and who does not receive the revealer, a question of insiders and outsiders that recurs throughout the narrative.

(7) There came a woman of Samaria to draw water. Jesus said to her, "Give me a drink." (8) For his disciples had gone away into the city to buy food. (9) The Samaritan woman said to him, "How is it that you, a Jew, ask a drink of me, a woman of Samaria?" For Jews have no dealings with Samaritans. (10) Jesus answered her, "If you knew the gift of God, and who it is that is saying to you, 'Give me a drink,' you would have asked him, and he would have given you living water." (11) The woman said to him, "Sir, you have nothing to draw with, and the well is deep; where do you get that living water? (12) Are you greater than our father Jacob, who gave us the well, and drank from it himself, and his sons, and his cattle?" (13) Jesus said to her, "Every one who drinks of this water will thirst again, (14) but whoever drinks of the water that I shall give him will never thirst; the water that I shall give him will become in him a spring of water welling up to eternal life." (15) The woman said to him, "Sir, give me this water, that I may not thirst, nor come here to draw." (16) Jesus said to her, "Go, call your husband, and come here." (17) The woman answered him, "I have no husband." Jesus said to her, "You are right in saying 'I have no husband'; (18) for you have had five husbands, and he whom you now have is not your husband; this you said truly." (19) The woman said to him, "Sir, I perceive that you are a prophet. (20) Our fathers worshiped on this mountain; and you say that in Jerusalem is the place where men ought to worship." (21) Jesus said to her, "Woman, believe me, the hour is coming when neither on this mountain nor in Jerusalem will you worship the Father. (22) You worship what you do not know; we worship what we know, for salvation is from the Jews. (23) But the hour is coming, and now is, when the true worshipers will worship the Father in spirit and truth, for such the Father seeks to worship him. (24) God is spirit, and those who worship him must worship in spirit and truth." (25) The woman said to him, "I know that Messiah is coming (he who is called Christ); when he comes, he will show us all things." (26) Jesus said to her, "I who speak to you am he." (John 4:7–26)

The dialogue between Jesus and the Samaritan woman is the longest single section of John 4:4–42. This narrative consists of thirteen speeches, one of the longest dialogues in the Gospel.[19] As noted above, it divides itself into two sections, each section marked by a request/command by Jesus.

John 4:7–15. These verses present a tightly composed scene. The scene opens with the arrival of the Samaritan woman at the well to draw water. The evangelist is not concerned that she has come to draw water at a rather unusual hour; the temporal reference is made in relation to Jesus' arrival at the well, not hers. What is important for the story is that the woman is a Samaritan and that she is prepared to draw water.

The dialogue begins with Jesus' request for water, "Give me a drink." As is so typical in Johannine dialogues, Jesus is the initiator of the conversation. He is not the one asked, as is normally the case in synoptic dialogues, but he is the one who does the asking.[20] Verse 6 has already provided one rationale for Jesus' request for water, but the evangelist provides even further justification in v. 8: not only is Jesus tired, but he is also now sitting alone at the well with no one to give him water. His disciples have gone to the town to buy food, so the only possible source of nourishment and refreshment is the Samaritan woman who stands before him.[21] The beginning of the story appears logical enough.

Yet is this request for water as simple as it appears? The Samaritan woman's response in v. 9 indicates that it is not. She responds in amazement, "How is it that you, a Jew, ask a drink from me, a woman of Samaria?" The woman's question establishes a clear division between herself and Jesus, a division reflected in the well-balanced language: you, a Jew/from me, a Samaritan woman.[22] The words which break the symmetry of this verse are the astonished interrogative "How is it?" (pōs) and the source of the woman's astonishment, the request for a drink. With an economy of expression, John has indicated both what is at issue for the woman and her sense of the dissonance of the situation.

The aside in v. 9c seeks to clarify this dissonance by explaining, at least on the surface level, why the woman is astonished. Yet one has to stop and ask if this aside which describes Samaritan/Jewish relations is necessary to render the woman's reaction comprehensible. The precise wording of her own statement establishes and underscores the polarity between Jews and Samaritans to such an extent that v. 9c almost appears superfluous. It is not necessary to assume, however, that it is a later editorial gloss,[23] because it is quite in keeping with the Fourth Evangelist's literary technique to insert often his own explicit, summarizing comments into the narrative.[24]

Most of the debate about v. 9c has focused on the type of Samaritan/ Jewish relationship it presupposes,[25] not on its function in the narrative. If we read v. 9c seriously as the evangelist's own comment on the Samaritan woman's response, then we may be able to arrive at a better idea of its function.

By enlarging upon what the Samaritan woman has already made clear, the evangelist appears to direct the reader's attention to the issue of Jewish/Samaritan relations and the breach of conduct that is taking place in the scene. But for the evangelist, and for the reader who has moved through the Gospel with him, the encounter between Jesus and the Samaritan woman is not just the encounter between *a* Jew and a Samaritan. The "How is it?" for the evangelist does not ultimately arise because Jews and Samaritans do not have relations with one another, but from the fact that the Jew who asks the woman for water is not just any Jew; he is the King of the Jews (19:19), the one in whose name we ask (14:14, 16:24). The dissonance for John arises when the woman understands Jesus' request only in terms of Samaritan/Jewish relations—she is unaware of the identity of the Jew with whom she speaks. This is not to relativize the Samaritan/ Jewish aspect of v. 9 (see further development in the narrative, especially 4:22 and 42), but to suggest that John uses v. 9c to accomplish two different things at once. What he says at the literal level is and remains valid, but the statement as an ironic understatement of the situation also has another meaning that points toward the larger central issue of Jesus' identity.

That this is the direction in which John wants to lead the reader is indicated by Jesus' response to the Samaritan woman in v. 10. He does not answer her in terms of Samaritan/Jewish relations but in terms of his identity: "If you knew the gift of God and who it is that is saying to you, 'Give me a drink,' you would have asked him and he would have given you living water." Jesus does not give a direct answer to the woman's "How?" but instead indicates that she herself could have the ability to answer her own question ("If you knew . . . ").

Of particular importance for understanding the dynamics of the narrative and what is being asked of the woman is Jesus' description of himself: "who it is that is saying to you *(ho legōn soi),* 'Give me a drink,' . . . ." Jesus does not refer to himself in general terms, but in terms specific to the woman's present situation. It is the recognition of the true identity of the very person with whom she is engaged in conversation that could result in their dramatic role reversal. With its emphasis on Jesus' speaking, the expression *ho legōn soi* also seems to be an early indication of the revelatory dimension of the text.[26] This aspect will be confirmed for the reader from the retrospective vantage point of v. 26.

The total role reversal that the Samaritan woman's recognition of Jesus would accomplish is underscored by the concrete language in which it is described. Again it is language specific to the woman's situation. John repeats the second person pronoun "you" *(su)* to draw attention to the new role which the woman would fill. Her potential new relation to Jesus is further emphasized in the central verbs from vv. 7 and 9, "ask" *(aiteō)*, "give" *(didomi)*, and "drink" *(pinō)*, which are repeated in v. 10 but are attributed to the opposite character. The woman who was initially astonished by Jesus' request would become the one who requests, and she who was asked to give would be the one given to.

The object of the woman's request is also transformed by Jesus. The water which the woman will receive is living water *(hydōr zōn)*, an ambiguous expression which can be understood both as "living" water and as spring, that is, "running" water. The expression's structural relation to the gift of God signals the reader, if not the woman, that Jesus does not have simple running water in mind,[27] but the precise referent of living water remains open. The woman will not be able to interpret living water correctly until she can recognize the identity of the person with whom she speaks.

In v. 10, therefore, Jesus does not explicitly supply the woman with the knowledge that she needs to make this next move in the dialogue. Instead of telling the Samaritan woman who he is, he leaves her with a question.[28] It is a question, however, which says more than a declarative statement could. Through his conditional statement, Jesus asks the woman to reassess her perception of the present situation. She assumes that she is in conversation with a thirsty Jew; this Jew informs her that if she knew both the gift of God and the identity of the person with whom she was speaking, she would recognize that she herself was the thirsty one.

This verse discloses that the conversation between Jesus and the Samaritan woman is being conducted on two levels simultaneously: one level as perceived by the woman and one as perceived by Jesus. These levels provide the basis of the irony of the dialogue, for they are at odds with one another. The clue given here by Jesus to his true identity is an invitation both to the woman and to the reader to grasp both levels of the conversation and their inherent contradictions and to move through the woman's level to Jesus'. As the dialogue unfolds, the Samaritan woman will struggle to communicate successfully with Jesus, a struggle precipitated by her not comprehending Jesus' invitation. As the reader watches the woman struggle with the two levels of the conversation, never moving completely from her starting place, the reader has this opening statement of Jesus as confirmation that he or she has correctly read the possibility of a second level. Verse 10 presents not only the goal of the narrative, to discover Jesus' identity, but also indicates how the narrative should be read to arrive at that goal.

Verses 11 and 12 are the first indication that the Samaritan woman has not comprehended the invitation offered by Jesus. She reacts to his statement purely on the original level of the conversation, that of drinking water, keying in on the ambiguous expression *hydōr zōn*. The woman's reaction and misunderstanding of Jesus' statement stem from her confident assessment of the situation: it is not credible to her that a man who has just asked her for water because he was unable to acquire any for himself ("Sir, you have nothing to draw with and the well is deep") should now offer her fresh running water. She therefore asks Jesus a question quite natural for the situation: "From where *(pothen)* do you have the living water?"

It is true that this question, like the "How is it?" in v. 9, registers a sense of incongruity at what Jesus says and does.[29] Yet the woman's "From where?" *(pothen)* actually reflects a much deeper ignorance on her part, as she asks one of the most ironically charged questions in the Gospel—the whence of Jesus and his gifts.[30] Throughout the Gospel, John contrasts Jesus' knowledge of his origin with the ignorance and false assumptions of his interlocutors.[31] Throughout Jesus knows himself to be "from above" *(anōthen)* and no one, including Nicodemus, understands (see esp. 3:31 and 8:23). Questions concerning the origin and source of Jesus' gifts reflect a similar contrast: 1:29,

3:8, 4:11, and 6:5 all ask about the whence of Jesus' gifts. In 1:48, Nathanael raises a related question about the source of Jesus' knowledge (*pothen* do you know me?). The Samaritan woman has asked a question that is plausible on both levels of the conversation—the question "from where" is as appropriate to ask of drinking water as it is of Jesus' gift of living water. The irony arises because the woman is only aware of the question's appropriateness on the first level; she does not know that she has asked a question of central importance for understanding Jesus' identity.

The woman's question in v. 12 focuses directly on Jesus' identity when she asks, "Are you greater than our father Jacob . . . ?" *(mē su meizōn ei tou patros hēmōn 'Iakōb).* This question is a universally recognized instance of Johannine irony.[32] The immediate source of its irony is clear: for John and most of his readers Jesus is of course greater than Jacob. John's use of *mē* here to introduce the question, a construction which anticipates a negative reply, underscores the ironic false assumption that the woman is making.[33] This is not the only occurrence of such irony in the Fourth Gospel. John 4:12 is verbally identical with the Jews' question in 8:53, "Are you greater than our father Abraham?" The question of Jesus' superiority to the patriarchs receives a consistently ironic treatment in the Gospel.[34]

The woman's question involves more than a general comparison between Jesus and Jacob, however.[35] Her question about Jesus' identity is intimately connected with this offer of living water. Since Jesus has no visible means with which to draw water, the woman's comparison with Jacob seems to imply that only a miracle similar to the one performed by Jacob at Haran could produce the water. The woman patriotically defends Jacob (*our* father Jacob) and the magnitude of his gift by stressing the numbers that drank at his well: not only did Jacob himself drink from it, but also his sons and his cattle. That Jesus would be able to equal or surpass such a water supply is incomprehensible to the woman. Her response to Jesus' offer is to question, and her questions ironically reveal an ignorance both of the nature of the proffered gift and of the identity of the speaker.

Jesus does not answer either of the woman's questions directly, but, as we saw with v. 10, indirection often says more than a direct statement could. Jesus ironically undercuts the woman's speech, pointing out that the abundance of the water supply is not a sign of superiority, but rather of inferiority when compared with the water offered by Jesus.[36] The comparison which the woman initiated between Jacob's and Jesus' gifts is now completed by Jesus: "Every one who drinks of this water will thirst again, but whoever drinks of the water that I shall give him will never thirst; the water that I shall give him will become in him a spring of water welling up to eternal life."

As in v. 10, Jesus once again draws the woman's attention to their conversation on two different levels. She speaks quite literalistically about water and well, whereas Jesus moves beyond such literalism to metaphor about water and well. The difference between these wells and their water is described in terms of their effect on thirst, the pretext under which the dialogue was first initiated (v. 7). The language of vv. 13 and 14 highlights the different effects of the waters: drinking from Jacob's well is expressed by a present participle *(pas ho pinōn)*, thus indicating that the action is indeed one which is repeated, while drinking of the water offered by Jesus is expressed by an aorist subjunctive *(hos d'an piȩ̄)*, thus indicating a completed, self-contained act.[37] This description of the two waters and wells also indirectly answers the question of Jesus' relation to Jacob. The juxtaposition of "every one who drinks" with the woman's list of those who drank from Jacob's well, including Jacob himself ("and he drank from it himself"), clearly places Jacob among those who continue to thirst because they have not drunk the water offered by Jesus.[38]

The description of the water offered by Jesus contains three central themes: (1) that the water will quench thirst forever, (2) that it will become a well/spring within each individual, and (3) that this well/spring will spring up into eternal life.[39] Verses 13–14 therefore make explicit what one only sensed implicitly in v. 10: the living water which Jesus offers is not drinking water.[40] The two conflicting levels of the conversation are also made explicit. What is central to the dynamics of the narrative, however, is not that Jesus simply points out the kind of water that he is *really* talking about. If that were the case, the dialogue would be superfluous and a discourse would suffice. Instead, the give and take between Jesus and the woman is essential to John's portrait of Jesus as revealer. The woman's struggle to move from her vantage point to Jesus', to understand fully Jesus' words and thereby discover who Jesus is, enables the reader to experience Jesus and his revelation in a way that would be impossible if reading straight discourse.

Verse 15 underscores this point. If the scene had ended with v. 14, the reader would have left the narrative with some sense of satisfaction—and possibly smug security—after having read this wisdom-like saying about living water, thirst, and eternal life. The function of the preceding narrative (vv. 7–12) would appear to be that of providing a backdrop for this teaching of Jesus, much like many of the synoptic narratives. With its words about eternity *(eis ton aiōna)* and eternal life *(eis zoēn aiōnion)*, how could anyone miss the point that we are dealing with theological discourse? The dialogue does not end with v. 14, however, and the woman's response in v. 15 indicates that someone indeed has "missed the point."

The Samaritan woman's response begins as an appropriate response to Jesus' words, "Sir, give me this water," but goes awry when she clarifies the reason for her request, "in order that I may not thirst nor come here to draw." The woman has not moved with Jesus! She has understood his words in part, that his water is better than the water in Jacob's well, but she does not understand why. She interprets Jesus' words about the quenching of thirst as referring solely to physical thirst, and requests the gift of water from Jesus so that she will no longer be obliged to come to the well to draw water.

With v. 15 we therefore end up where we began—with a request for water. The request with which the dialogue opened, "give me a drink" *(dos moi pein)*, is now ironically placed in the mouth of the other dialogue partner, "give me this water" *(dos moi touto to hydōr)*. The evangelist's careful use of the verb *didōmi* conveys the dynamics of the dialogue. The repetition of the imperative *dos* signifies that just as the woman was ignorant of Jesus' true identity when *he* was the petitioner (v. 9), she is still ignorant of it now that *she* is the petitioner.

It would be incorrect to say that the woman's perspective has not changed at all. Instead of viewing Jesus as an ordinary, if somewhat socially ignorant Jew, she now views him as a miracle worker who can provide her with extraordinary water. But to say that the woman has fulfilled one part of Jesus' condition in v. 10 would also be incorrect.[41] Although by her request for water the woman is ostensibly doing exactly what Jesus had earlier said she should do, she does not know what she is asking for nor of whom she is asking it. Her ignorance highlights the irony of her response, for the comprehending reader knows that the woman is making the correct request in spite of herself.

The irony of the situation does not arise only because the Samaritan woman has misunderstood Jesus, nor only because she has failed to grasp the true meaning of Jesus' water and his words. Rather the irony results because at one level the woman *has* correctly understood. If we recall that for a "sentence to be properly ironic it must be possible to imagine some group of readers taking it quite literally,"[42] the very presence of the Samaritan woman and her responses in this early part of the dialogue fill this need. She takes things quite literally, and from her perspective, a coherent dialogue occurs.[43] The interplay between Jesus and his dialogue partners—the Samaritan woman here, the disciples later—dramatizes the two conflicting levels of meaning that the reader must grasp simultaneously in order to interpret irony correctly. As the contrast between vv. 14 and 15 shows, one level of meaning is incomplete without the other.

Since both levels of meaning are fully embodied in the text, this means that the reader must constantly move with the text as he or she attempts to read the two levels in concert. In this way the reader is drawn into the text. It is interesting to note that in a text in which the reader is constantly asked and challenged to make decisions about how to interpret the scene being played before him or her, one of the central characters in this scene seems incapable of making such a decision herself. At the beginning of the dialogue the woman makes no decision as to whether or not she should give Jesus water (she neither refuses him nor serves him).[44] When at the end of this section of the dialogue the woman finally does make a decision ("Give me"), from the point of view of the comprehending reader it is the *wrong* decision. The woman and the reader have followed the same series of steps (vv. 10, 13, 14) but have arrived at different places.

The irony of the woman's decision is further underscored by Jesus' (and the evangelist's) silence in response to it. The evangelist lets the woman's statement stand as is, without directly commenting on it or correcting the woman's perception of living water. The commentary comes from its juxtaposition with vv. 16–26.

John 4:16–26. The break between vv. 15 and 16 is abrupt. Jesus suddenly shifts the discussion from living water to the woman's husband with his command, "Go, call your husband and come here," and the juxtaposition is jarring to the reader. Commentators have proposed many reasons for this change of topic in their attempts to impose an external logical structure on the text,[45] but the narrative itself provides ample explanation for this sudden juxtaposition.

The dialogue in vv. 16–26 plays off the woman's misperception of both the nature of the gift and the giver. In v. 15 the woman asks for water so that she will not have to return to the well *(mēde dierchōmai enthade antlein)*. In v. 16, however, Jesus asks her to do that very thing: he sends her away after her husband, but then tells her to come back to the well *(elthe enthade)*. [46] The juxtaposition of these two uses of *enthade* creates an irony that focuses the reader's attention on the different meanings of "place" in the dialogue. The ironic use of "from where" *(pothen)* in the woman's question concerning the source of living water (v. 11) has already indicated that she is ignorant of the origin of Jesus' gifts; Jesus' throwing her own request back at her underscores that ignorance here. The Samaritan woman has identified the gift of water with a place, and does not understand that the gift is dependent on the giver, not on any well.

The dialogue that ensues between Jesus and the woman concerning her marital status is intended by John to shed further light on the person of Jesus as revealer. The woman's response to Jesus' request seems straightforward enough ("I do not have a husband") and provides a legitimate reason for her inability to comply with Jesus' words. Jesus' reply, however, causes the reader to think again: "You are right in saying, 'I do not have a husband'; for you have had five husbands, and he whom you now have is not your husband; this you said truly."[47] Jesus and the reader have heard/read the same statement and interpreted it to mean completely different things. From Jesus' perspective, and in retrospect for the reader, the woman's statement is a masterful example of ironic understatement. What she says is true but is at odds with what she means. Similarly, Jesus' own response begins as an affirmation of the reader's original interpretation of the woman's statement. It is not until Jesus indicates *why* the woman has spoken truthfully that the reader is able to see the full significance of both speeches. If the woman's statement is ironic understatement, Jesus' is ironic overstatement[48]—his words are also true, but their manifest meaning is in conflict with their intended meaning. The emphasis which Jesus places on the veracity of the woman's statements is such overt irony that it borders on biting sarcasm.[49]

Jesus' revelation of his knowledge of her true marital status leads the woman to declare him to be a prophet (v. 19). One could compare the woman's response to that of Nathanael in 1:47–51; from an unexpected demonstration of knowledge on Jesus' part comes a profession of Jesus' identity. There is an important difference, however, between this scene and the Nathanael scene. John does not just provide the reader with a demonstration of Jesus' omniscience, as is the case in 1:47–51. Instead he involves the reader in every step from naive ignorance to enlightenment, so that the reader can make the discovery for himself or herself. In vv. 16–19 the *reader* is the one who is on the outside, while Jesus and the woman are the insiders who possess the true information about her marital status. Both the reader and the woman are surprised by Jesus' revelation in v. 18, but they are surprised for different reasons. The woman is surprised because Jesus has seen through her understatement to the truth, while the reader is surprised both because of Jesus' ability to discern the truth and because of the truth itself. The reader is made to feel the impact of Jesus' omniscience in a way that a declarative statement could not convey (cf. 2:24–25). From the reader's perspective, this short exchange is one of the most engaging in the dialogue.

The woman's profession of Jesus as a prophet, while not a recognition of his full identity, is a step in the right direction.[50] It also provides the basis for her statements about the correct place of worship in v. 20. As in the case of the break between vv. 15 and 16, many scholars have puzzled over the rationale for the introduction of the worship theme in vv. 20–24. Attempts to explain the introduction of this theme range from minor to major psychologizing[51] and are often based on a caricatured view of the "personality" and function of the woman.[52] All such attempts ignore the evidence provided by the narrative itself. John does not separate v. 19 from v. 20, but both are part of the same speech by the Samaritan woman. As she stands at or near a Samaritan holy place with someone whom she assumes to be a Jewish prophet, she puts before him a central issue of both Samaritan and Jewish worship.[53] Her words about worship are therefore both textually and semantically linked to her acknowledgment of Jesus as prophet.

For the first time in the dialogue, the woman is the initiator of the topic of conversation, so the issue of worship is put forward in her terms. Her indirect query about the right place to worship reflects the same polarity of thought with which she began: *our fathers* versus *you* in v. 20 parallels *you, a Jew* versus *me, a Samaritan woman* in v. 9. The woman still understands the relationship of the two dialogue partners as that of Samaritan versus Jew. Jesus picks up her terms and polarities when he begins his response, but in the course of his speech he will transform and transcend them.

Verses 21–24 constitute Jesus' longest speech in the dialogue. The words with which he begins, "Believe me, woman," mean the same thing as the more customary "Truly, truly I say to you."[54] They are an indication that what Jesus is about to say is something to which the woman should devote her attention. Jesus then proceeds to speak with words that point to a time in the future, "the hour is coming when." The woman presented the issue of worship in terms of past *(prosekynēsan)* and present *(estin ho topos hopou proskynein dei);* Jesus begins to answer her in terms of the future.

Jesus' words in v. 21 reflect a technique that we have seen before in the dialogue: the words of one speech are repeated in another (vv. 7, 9, and 10; 7 and 15; 15 and 16; 17 and 18). Here Jesus repeats the woman's statement in order to refute it: "neither on this mountain nor in Jerusalem will you worship the Father." It is important to note that the woman's statement in v. 20 did not indicate *what* is being worshipped. Jesus introduces the object of worship by supplying "the Father." This addition is important not only in relation to what follows—as it is one of the central elements in Jesus' discussion of worship—but also in relation to what precedes. The use of *patēr* here is the culmination of a theme which John has developed ironically throughout the dialogue.[55]

"Father" *(patēr)* is first introduced indirectly in the narrative when the evangelist describes Sychar as near the land which Jacob gave *to his son Joseph.* The Samaritan woman explicitly mentions Jacob as father in v. 12, and his "children" are expanded from his own flesh and blood to include all the Samaritans. The next use of *patēr* (v. 20) expands the meaning in a different way. Jacob, and all the Samaritan ancestors, are included under the rubric "our fathers." John subtly changes the meaning of father in this text, from the father of one son to the collective Samaritan fathers. All these referents for father are dramatically undercut, however, by the one expression of Jesus: you will worship *the Father.* By repetition and juxtaposition John has ironically shown that the Samaritan woman has no idea who the Father is.

This may be what lies behind the problematic saying of v. 22, "You worship what you do not know, we worship what we know, because salvation is from the Jews." In the context of the dialogue the woman has demonstrated that she really *does not know* what she worships; Jesus was the one who supplied the object of worship in v. 21. This would suggest that the you/we polarity refers, as it has throughout the dialogue, to Samaritans and Jews.[56] In the light of vv. 9 and 20, it is not at all surprising that Jesus identifies himself with the Jews. At this point in the speech, Jesus is still responding to the concern of the Samaritan woman in her own terms, and *she* broached the worship issue in terms of this polarity.

Verse 22b is one of the most debated verses in John 4. The central issue is whether or not it is a later editorial gloss.[57] The main reason for reading it as a gloss is that in light of what precedes it, "nor in Jerusalem," and what follows, a discussion of worship which transcends national bounds, this comment seems not only disruptive but contradictory. Even some authors who analyze the rest of John 4:4–42 as a literary unity reject this verse as a later gloss.[58] Two preliminary observations argue against rejecting this verse as a gloss. First, in vv. 21 and 23–24 Jesus is talking about the eschatological hour; in v. 22 he is discussing the present reality. Second, if one is going to reject

v. 22b as a gloss, then one should probably reject all of v. 22, since the you/we polarity of the first half establishes a similar nationalistic bias. The points of contact between vv. 20–21 and v. 22, however, argue against rejecting the whole verse out of hand.

There are more basic reasons for accepting v. 22b as an essential part of the dialogue. First, we must recall that Jesus is still responding to the woman's polarities; he is putting the issue in her terms. But second, and more important, in the context of both the Samaritan narrative and the full Gospel, this verse is not only possible but comprehensible. Verse 22b says only that salvation is *from (ek)* the Jews; it says nothing about who receives it. Salvation does originate from God's "own" people, the Jews, but in the Fourth Gospel it is the non-Jews who recognize and accept it.[59] One need only turn to the prologue to see how central this thought is to John: "He came to his own home, and his own people received him not" (1:11). There may be an ironic undertone to John's use of "salvation is from the Jews" here, since in the Fourth Gospel one of the themes which receives consistently ironic treatment is that of the Jews' rejection of the Messiah for whom they are waiting.[60] The immediate context of the Samaria narrative lends support to an ironic reading. The offer of salvation made by Jesus (the Jew) has just been rejected by the Jew Nicodemus but will be accepted by the Samaritans with no national strings attached (4:42). Immediately following the Samaritan's acceptance of Jesus, a court official in Galilee will also accept this "Jewish" salvation.[61]

In v. 22, therefore, Jesus takes the woman's Samaritan/Jew polarity to its extreme, but in v. 23 all that changes. The "but" with which v. 23 begins marks a decisive turning point in Jesus' speech. First, the time frame for the new worship is now different. In v. 21 the hour when the mode of worship would change is coming; in v. 23 it is not only coming, but *now is.* The *alla* ("but") of v. 23a is reinforced by the *kai gar* ("for even") of v. 23b. The eschatological moment is present, and that provides a totally new perspective from which to view the question of worship. The worship of the Father, briefly introduced in v. 21, is developed fully here. Worship of the Father in spirit and truth does not point to an internal, spiritualized worship that thereby makes the place of worship irrelevant. Instead it points to a true and full worship of the Father that reflects a full knowledge of who the Father is and full communion with the Father ("God is spirit, and those who worship God must worship in spirit and truth"). The historical problem of Jewish versus Samaritan worship is transformed into a statement of the eschatological encounter with divine reality. This eschatological mode of worship is possible now ("and now is") because Jesus and the gift of his revelation make the spirit accessible. It is only through recognition of Jesus' identity and entry into relationship with him that one becomes a true worshipper.[62] That God seeks those who worship in spirit and truth (v. 23b) underscores that this worship is indeed present and accessible through one's present relationship with Jesus.[63]

Verse 23 also marks a second turning point in Jesus' speech. The ironic interplay between the woman's terminology and Jesus' appropriation of it is abandoned in these verses for a more discursive style. In vv. 23–24 Jesus no longer responds to the woman according to her categories but introduces his own terms into the conversation. The different literary mode employed here helps to emphasize the shift from the ordinary present to the eschatological present. The nature and function of the second level of the conversation (and existence) towards which Jesus has attempted to move the woman throughout the dialogue (vv. 10, 13, 14, 16) is once again made explicit here. And more importantly, it is made explicit as simultaneously operative with the manifest level of the conversation and existence. The Samaritan woman, and through her the reader, is told in the most direct language of the dialogue to date that true worship, this new relationship with God as Father, is present *now.* As in v. 10, the woman is once again asked to reassess her perception of the situation in which she finds herself. Her understanding of present worship is at odds with the eschatologically present worship in the spirit proclaimed by Jesus. (The ironic tension between these two forms of worship is brought out by both characters' use of the expression "must worship" [*dei proskynein*] in vv. 20 and 24.) If the woman can recognize that she is speaking with the person who makes the eschatological age a present reality, she will be able to participate in the spirit as a true

71

worshipper. If not, the ironic distance between her perspective and Jesus' will remain.

The Samaritan woman does interpret one aspect of Jesus' speech correctly. She understands that he is talking about the eschatological age and she knows that this age is the age of the Messiah. What she misses, however, is the critical "and now is":[64] "I know that Messiah is coming (he who is called Christ); *when he comes,* he will show us all things."[65] With each of the woman's words, the irony of her perspective in relation to that of Jesus (and that of the evangelist and the comprehending reader) intensifies. As was the case with her reply in v. 15, v. 25 opens with words that are potentially appropriate as a response to Jesus. That she knows the Messiah is coming could follow logically from Jesus' words, but only if she adds "and now is."[66] Instead her words reflect the opposite perspective—*whenever (hotan)* that one comes. Not only has the Samaritan woman missed the significance of Jesus' words about the eschatological hour, she also does not realize that the person *of* whom she speaks is the person *with* whom she speaks. She does not recognize that the person who speaks with her has not only initiated the anticipated time of salvation but also represents it in his person.[67] And finally, after Jesus has announced "everything" with his proclamation of the eschatological worship in spirit and truth, the woman states that she still awaits this announcement. The Samaritan woman's words ironically show that she is open to the words of the Messiah, but that she has not made the crucial step which will lead to her recognition and acceptance of Jesus and his revelation.

Jesus answers the woman (v. 26) with his most direct statement of the dialogue: "I am, the one who speaks to you" (au. trans.) *(egō eimi, ho lalōn soi).* This statement provides the answer to the question which Jesus put before the Samaritan woman in v. 10: "who it is that speaks to you" *(ho legōn soi).* The association of these two verses leaves little doubt that this is an absolute *egō eimi,* that is, an *egō eimi* saying that is an unqualified revelation of Jesus' identity. John does not intend for us to supply the predicate from the woman's statement in v. 25.[68] Jesus is *not* confirming that he is the Messiah expected by the Samaritan woman but is using the *egō eimi* in its fullest sense to identify himself as God's revealer, the sent one of God (4:34). It is true that on one level Jesus does fulfill the Samaritan woman's messianic expectations, and this fulfillment creates another irony in the narrative that will be highlighted when the woman returns to town with word of Jesus. The use of the absolute *egō eimi*, however, shows that although Jesus incorporates aspects of Samaritan beliefs, he also transcends them. One cannot understand "who is the one speaking to you" until one relinquishes predetermined categories (e.g., Samaritan/Jew) and responds to Jesus in terms of Jesus' revelation. The ironic disjunction between what the Samaritan woman sees in Jesus and what Jesus presents to her signals to the reader that "as long as one tries to grasp Jesus as a Jew or a Greek or a Gnostic [or a Samaritan] or a traditional Christian would, [one] both succeeds and fails, for Jesus is the fulfillment of all these expectations, but he is caught up in none of them."[69]

Throughout the dialogue, John has let stand, often without explicit comment, two contradictory perceptions of the same event. The "correct" view is never allowed to stand in isolation. When Jesus makes an explicit statement (e.g., vv. 13 and 14, 23 and 24), John immediately undercuts it with the woman's response. The reader is left to decipher the relationship between the two perspectives and to choose between them. The ironic "double exposure" of Jesus' statements and the woman's responses allows for reader participation in the revelatory process in a way that declarative statements could not. It is for this reason that the *egō eimi* of v. 26 has such tremendous impact on the reader. The distance which John has allowed throughout the dialogue for the woman's and the reader's free movement toward Jesus is removed with this absolute statement of self-revelation. The reader is faced with a direct, definitive revelation of Jesus that calls for a type of decision different from that of the ironic interplay of the rest of the dialogue. Now the decision is only to affirm or deny. The reader is prepared to make this decision, however, only because she or he has been involved in the revelatory process of the earlier dialogue. The *egō eimi* is therefore experienced, not just recounted.

When Jesus declares himself as *egō eimi*, the ultimate revelation of the Samaria narrative has been made. The rest of the narrative is not anticlimactic, however, but provides confirmation of this revelation and places it in a new light. As we shall see, the disciples were not present for this revelation. They must therefore be drawn into the revelatory dynamic themselves.

> (27) Just then his disciples came. They marveled that he was talking with a woman, but none said, "What do you wish?" or, "Why are you talking with her?" (28) So the woman left her water jar, and went away into the city, and said to the people, (29) "Come, see a man who told me all that I ever did. Can this be the Christ?" (30) They went out of the city and were coming to him. (John 4:27–30)

John 4:27–30. This transition scene has two structural points of contact with the preceding dialogue. First, the reader is not surprised by the disciples' reappearance, because v. 8 had given reason to expect that they would return. Second, the disciples' arrival is immediately followed by the woman's departure, the inverse of the relationship between vv. 7 and 8.

This scene also has more substantive links with vv. 7–26. Although the disciples are amazed that Jesus is conversing with a woman, they do not make their amazement known ("But none said . . ."). This is quite a contrast with the behavior of the woman, who voiced her thoughts when anything was startling or incongruous. Although one might explain the disciples' silence as the result of reverence or awe toward their master,[70] the comparison with the woman's behavior provides an explanation that is more in keeping with the dynamics of the narrative.

Even though the woman made wrong choices in her conversation with Jesus, one important aspect of her responses was that through her often blunt questioning she remained engaged in dialogue with Jesus. As we commented earlier, such engagement and participation are central elements in the revelatory process. The disciples, by contrast, do not question at this juncture and therefore keep themselves removed from immediate engagement with Jesus. At this moment in the narrative they are "outsiders," mere observers of the scene that is taking place.[71] Their status as outsiders is ironically underscored by the questions to Jesus they leave unvoiced: "What do you seek?" or "Why are you talking with her?" These questions touch at the heart of Jesus' dialogue with the Samaritan woman and, importantly, touch at *both levels.* Verses 7 and 10 supply coherent answers to these questions. The question "What do you seek?" has an additional irony in its context. Jesus has just told the Samaritan woman that the Father seeks those who worship him in spirit and truth, and now the disciples are somewhat incredulous that Jesus could be seeking anything from this woman.[72] The ultimate irony of these questions, which highlights the disciples' ignorance and disengagement, is that the reader can answer both questions on both levels. For the moment, the reader is more involved with Jesus' revelation than his disciples are.

If v. 22b is one of the most debated verses of the narrative, then v. 28 is the most intriguing to commentators and has inspired some of the most imaginative, if somewhat dubious, exegesis of any of the verses. The description of the woman's departure is what intrigues commentators: "So the woman left her water jar, and went away into the city." Why does John mention that she left her water jar? The attempts to answer this question often range from the sublime to the ridiculous. In recent historical-critical interpretation of this verse, for example, we read that the Samaritan woman left the jar so that Jesus could drink from it in her absence,[73] or that this detail indicates that the *hydria* would be useless for the living water.[74] The problem with such interpretations is that they are not supported by evidence in the text and do not take the narrative context of the verse seriously. The most reasonable explanation of this verse, and the one which the text itself supports, is that this reference to the jar indicates that the woman is going to return.[75] Most commentators who propose this interpretation, however, base their view solely on the evidence of v. 28 and not on the larger narrative, and their views thus appear to be as conjectural as those cited above. In the context of the total narrative, however, it becomes clear that the function of v. 28 is identical with that of v. 8: the details about going for food and leaving the water jar both indicate that the character who is moving off-stage is not disappearing forever. Both details prepare the reader for the character's return. Verses 8 and 28 have another complementary function: v. 8 introduces the theme of the second dialogue, *food,* into the scene with the woman,[76] and v. 28 continues the theme of the first dialogue, *water,* into the scene with the disciples.

When the woman arrives in the town, she brings the townspeople word of her encounter with Jesus: "Come, see a man who told me all that I ever did. This couldn't be the Christ, could it?" (au. trans.). The invitation to come and see Jesus is one which the reader of the Fourth Gospel has already encountered twice. In 1:39 Jesus responds to the question of two of John the Baptist's disciples, "Where are you staying?" with the reply, "Come and see." In the same narrative, Philip responds to Nathanael's question about Jesus with the reply "Come and see" (1:46).[77] The invitation to come and see Jesus is therefore an important step in understanding who Jesus is—it is the invitation to participate. This invitation is important, because it is only when one participates and enters into the revelatory dynamic that one can come to know who Jesus is. It is an ironic invitation in the mouth of the Samaritan woman, because she was able to see so little in the course of her conversation with Jesus. It is the correct invitation, but she offers it unknowingly.

The irony of her invitation intensifies when we observe the woman's description of Jesus. Her recognition of him is not based on his words about worship nor on his direct self-revelation but on his prophetic announcement of her marital status.[78] On one level she is of course correct, Jesus did tell her "all" that she ever did. But he also told her, like the Messiah she expects, "all things" (*hapanta*, v. 25). The irony arises when we compare the woman's understanding of "everything" with Jesus' statements.[79]

The last words spoken by the woman in the narrative contain her tentative confession of Jesus—"This couldn't be the Christ, could it?" (*mēti houtos estin ho christos*, v. 29). The *mēti* with which this statement begins is difficult to pin down; it is not a denial, but neither is it a full affirmation.[80] In light of the bold *egō eimi* of v. 26, it is difficult to see how anyone could respond so tentatively. In the context of the narrative, however, this tentativeness has an important function. Because it is not a definite assertion, it leaves room for individual response. In reflecting on the woman's question, the reader is drawn back to Jesus' own self-revelation.[81]

The conclusion of the transition scene, v. 30, functions analogously to vv. 8, 27, and 28. It signals the return of one set of characters and reminds the reader that the action of the narrative is being conducted on two fronts.[82] The very language of the verse, "They went out of the city and were coming to him," indicates that the action is occurring simultaneously with the scene between Jesus and his disciples. The imperfect form—*erchonto* ("were coming")—implies that the Samaritans are in the process of coming to Jesus but have not yet arrived. One cast of characters can be seen impinging on the other, and the interrelationship of the two is thus felt more strongly than ever before by the reader.[83] The impending arrival of the Samaritans is a tangible factor in the conversation between Jesus and his disciples.[84]

> (31) Meanwhile the disciples besought him, saying, "Rabbi, eat." (32) But he said to them, "I have food to eat of which you do not know." (33) So the disciples said to one another, "Has any one brought him food?" (34) Jesus said to them, "My food is to do the will of him who sent me, and to accomplish his work. (35) Do you not say, 'There are yet four months, then comes the harvest'? I tell you, lift up your eyes, and see how the fields are already white for harvest. (36) He who reaps receives wages, and gathers fruit for eternal life, so that sower and reaper may rejoice together. (37) For here the saying holds true, 'One sows and another reaps.' (38) I sent you to reap that for which you did not labor; others have labored, and you have entered into their labor." (John 4:31–38)

John 4:31–34. The "meanwhile" with which v. 31 begins directs the reader's attention back to the well as the narrative focus returns to Jesus and his dialogue partners. This dialogue between Jesus and his disciples is one of Jesus' few private conversations with them in the Fourth Gospel, outside of the farewell discourses.[85] As was the case in the dialogue with the Samaritan woman, this new section of the dialogue begins with an imperative, "Rabbi, eat *(phage)*." In contrast to the first dialogue, however, the imperative is used by the disciples, not by Jesus. The disciples' particular request provides a link with the preceding narrative, for it follows naturally from the information provided about them in v. 8.

The disciples are therefore the initiators of this conversation. Despite this role, Jesus' own comments really set the tone and determine the flow of the conversation. His response to the disciples, "I have food to eat of which you do not know," introduces a dynamic identical with that in the earlier dialogue. Just as the woman's comments about living water ironically revealed her ignorance of Jesus' identity, the disciples' comment about Jesus' food (v. 33) ironically reveals that they too are in need of knowledge. Jesus subsequently supplies this knowledge in the verses that follow.

In v. 31 the disciples address Jesus as rabbi, thereby drawing attention to their pupil/teacher relationship.[86] This relationship is underscored in v. 32 by Jesus' use of the phrase, "of which you do not know." In v. 27 the disciples' unvoiced questions had demonstrated their lack of knowledge; now Jesus explicitly draws attention to their ignorance. This phrase also establishes important links between the disciples and the Samaritan woman. The ironic interplay between Jesus and the Samaritan woman began with Jesus' statement of the woman's lack of knowledge ("If you knew . . . "). Like the disciples, the woman's own behavior had first demonstrated this lack of knowledge, through her reaction to Jesus' request for water (v. 9). Jesus' subsequent statement of her ignorance contained an invitation for her to see his categories ("I am, the one who speaks with you") within her categories (the one who says to you: "give me a drink"). The reader, attuned to the patterns of this narrative, recognizes a similar invitation in Jesus' declaration of the disciples' ignorance. The disciples are invited to see Jesus' categories (v. 34) as simultaneously operative with their own (vv. 27, 33), to see both levels of meaning at once. Verse 32 contains an anticipatory irony for the reader, for he or she is able to see this invitation while the disciples cannot.

The irony of the disciples' situation emerges fully in v. 33. From the disciples' perspective, the fact that Jesus already has food is surprising but not beyond the realm of logical plausibility: "So the disciples said to one another, 'Has anyone brought him food?' (mē tis ēnenken autǭ phagein)." The mē with which this question begins (the particle anticipating a negative response) indicates that the disciples already have *their* answer in mind, and thus ironically marks the false assumption that they are making.[87] Their question reflects the same perspective as that of the woman's questions in vv. 11 and 12. Just as the woman was able to see only one meaning of *hydōr zōn,* not both, the disciples can only understand *brōsis* as the food that they have

78

brought from town. They therefore assume that another person has taken their role and supplied Jesus with food, without sensing that something else is at issue in Jesus' words.

The reader, however, senses what the disciples do not. The reader, although not knowing exactly what Jesus means by *brōsis* (Jesus must supply the precise referent in v. 34), does know that Jesus means more than ordinary food and can therefore judge the disciples' question as completely inadequate in response to Jesus. The irony of v. 33 arises because the reader is able to grasp that which the disciples appear to be incapable of grasping.[88] The reader is able to understand *both* what Jesus says *and* what he means. For the moment the reader, as a result of his or her participation in the revelatory dynamics of the narrative, stands closer to Jesus' revelation than the disciples do. Jesus' words in v. 34, however, will eliminate the distance between the reader and the disciples.

John 4:34 is to this dialogue what 4:26 was to the first: it points to Jesus as God's revealer and the sent one of God. Verse 34 focuses on Jesus' *function* as constitutive of his identity: "My food *(brōma)* is that I do the will of the one who sent me and that I complete his work *(ergon)*." The food which Jesus is talking about here is not the food that he offers to others (cf. 6:27), nor is it Jesus himself (cf. the use of bread [*artos*] in 6:35), but it is Jesus' own food. This may account for the shift from *brōsis* in v. 32 to *brōma* in v. 34.[89] John's introduction of a new term signals that Jesus is introducing a new category that must be distinguished from the disciples' *brōsis.*[90]

Jesus' description of his food is a crystallization of Johannine christology: *brōma* appears as a metaphorical manifestation of Jesus' divine commission and of the working interrelationship of Jesus and God. Jesus is sustained by doing the will and the work of the one who sent him. There is an additional emphasis on Jesus' role in completing that work: "and that I complete his work" (cf. 5:36, 17:4). Verse 34 draws attention to the fact that any discussion of who Jesus is is meaningless without a discussion of what Jesus does, and vice versa.

This revelation given to the disciples has important links with the preceding narrative. First, it provides assistance in interpreting the *edei* ("he had to") of 4:4. From the retrospective vantage point of this presentation of Jesus' food, it seems impossible to deny that John intended theological necessity as well as geographical necessity to be understood by the reader. To be more precise, it becomes clear that geographical and theological necessity are inseparable—the necessity to pass through Samaria is part of doing God's will. Any reading of the *edei* that attempts to separate the geographical and the theological aspects is ironic from the perspective of the comprehending reader, because he or she knows that the two must be understood together. Second, this reading of 4:4, combined with 4:34, puts the whole dialogue with the Samaritan woman in a clearer light. Verses 7–26 present the reader with a specific illustration of the general principle of v. 34, of Jesus doing God's will and God's work.[91] The definition of God's *ergon* in 6:29, "This is the work of God, that you believe in the one whom God has sent," is quite applicable to the Samaria narrative. Finally, and perhaps most importantly, 4:34 gives body to Jesus' revelation in 4:26. Jesus interprets his own words with this statement on his sustaining and working unity with the one who sent him.

These words of Jesus to his disciples move them rapidly from a state of ignorance to one of knowledge. In the context of the full Gospel of John, one could say that they regain their status as insiders. To be more specific, this revelation solidifies their position, since they are given "inside knowledge" of which the Samaritan woman and her townspeople are unaware.[92] What is surprising about this shift in the narrative status of the disciples is not that it occurs, but how rapidly it occurs. Verses 26 and 34 are both direct statements by Jesus, but Jesus reveals himself with the *egō eimi* only after an involved revelatory exchange. For example, in 4:13–14 Jesus talked explicitly *about* living water but never supplied its precise referent. He left the possibility of the woman's misperception open. In 4:34 by contrast, the manner in which Jesus describes his food ("My food is . . . ") corrects the situation of crossed communication as soon as it appears. Jesus directly supplies the disciples with the information necessary to understand his identity, thereby eliminating the possibility of prolonged ironic interplay. When compared with the interplay of vv. 7–26, one wonders if a different communicative mode is being used here.

A close reading of the scene between Jesus and his disciples reveals that no genuine dialogue has occurred between the two parties.[93] In v. 27, as noted above, the disciples' questions remain unvoiced. In v. 33, the disciples speak to one another, not to Jesus. Jesus' response in v. 34 is not really a specific response to v. 33, but incorporates aspects of all the disciples' questions.[94] The dialogue with the disciples can therefore be seen as having discursive elements intermingled with the conversational and dialogical. This discursive character is expanded as the "dialogue" between Jesus and his disciples continues. In vv. 35–38 Jesus strings together a series of proverbs which either clarify or amplify what he said in v. 34. If we read vv. 34–38 as a unit, it appears that Jesus begins to speak in an *explanatory* mode. Although there is some irony in Jesus' application of these proverbs, nevertheless the reader still senses that he or she is dealing with a different mode of speaking.

The move from dialogical to discursive language in this scene is surprising at first, since the participation which the dialogical interplay of vv. 7–26 encouraged was seen as so essential to the revelatory mode. As we examine the proverbs in vv. 35–38 and then move on to the conclusion of the narrative, it will be important to ask ourselves if the different literary techniques which John uses in these sections reflect a different aspect of the revelatory mode.

John 4:35–38. The harvest proverbs and imagery develop naturally from v. 34.[95] Jesus has just spoken of his role in completing the work of the one who sent him; he then turns to a traditional biblical image for completion—the harvest.[96] Not only is the harvest a common image for completion, it is also an image for eschatological completion, making harvest imagery particularly appropriate in this context. The situation of vv. 31–34 is also continued in the harvest sayings: Jesus is still attempting to provide his disciples with the insight necessary to understand his work and his person.

Verse 35 begins with Jesus' presentation of the disciples' own viewpoint to them: "Do you not say, 'There are yet four months, then comes the harvest'?" The "Do you not say" with which this question begins implies that the question is rhetorical—Jesus knows that what he says is correct and does not expect the disciples to answer. The focus of the proverb which Jesus cites is on the waiting period between seedtime and harvest.[97] The second person plural pronoun *(humeis)* highlights the disciples as being among those who accept this proverb.

In v. 35b Jesus contrasts his perspective with that of the disciples —"Behold I say to you, lift up your eyes and see how the fields are white for harvest." The "Behold, I say to you" is adversative—the disciples believe that one must wait for the harvest; Jesus emphasizes that it is ready now. Jesus' words are a metaphorical illustration of what he said earlier to the Samaritan woman: "The hour is coming and now is." The traditional view (vv. 25, 35a) is that one must wait for the hour/harvest; in reality they are here now.[98] This focus on the eschatological future as present reality will soon tie all the agricultural imagery together.

Jesus' words in v. 35b contain a double exhortation to the disciples to *see* what is happening around them: "Lift up your eyes . . . see."[99] Jesus has earlier invited his interlocutors to see things correctly, but this invitation has always been implicit: the invitation itself often had to be discerned.[100] The double exhortation here stands in sharp contrast to those implicit invitations, because now Jesus gives an explicit charge to see. The double exhortation also emphasizes the object that the disciples are called to see. The disciples are called to pay particular attention to the specific situation in which they find themselves.[101] If we read the double exhortation in the context of v. 30 ("and they were coming to him"), then it seems that Jesus wants to direct the disciples' eyes toward the Samaritans who are approaching. The harvest refers not only to the ripened grain but to the "crop" of Samaritan believers. Jesus' work (see 4:34, 6:29, and above, p. 80) is culminated. The fields are indeed white for harvest.

Jesus is therefore speaking on two levels. What he says has both a literal and a figurative meaning. But do these levels relate to one another ironically? From one perspective the answer is no, Jesus is simply speaking of the Samaritans metaphorically. From another perspective, however, namely that of vv. 27–34, Jesus can be understood as speaking ironically. His words ironically underscore the disciples' misperception of his dialogue with the Samaritan woman and his food. The disciples have shown such a lack of insight that even now they do not realize what is happening around them: they cannot see the approaching Samaritans for what they are. Yet this irony does not function in the same way as irony functions in the dialogue with the Samaritan woman. Jesus does not linger in ironic speech. A situation of misunderstanding and miscommunication is not allowed to develop. The disciples are given no voice. Instead Jesus elaborates the workings and significance of the harvest.

In v. 35 the fields are white for harvest; in v. 36 the harvester is already at work.[102] The move from v. 35 to v. 36 thus involves a slight shift in the temporal framework. The activity of the harvester is linked with his relationship with the sower: "Already the harvester receives wages and gathers fruit for eternal life, so that the sower and the harvester may rejoice together." Who is the harvester, who is the sower? The emphasis on work, completion of work ("receives wages," "gathers fruit"), and the common purpose of harvester and sower in the work ("rejoice together") suggests that v. 36 is a metaphorical restatement of v. 34.[103] Jesus' food is to complete that work of the one who sent him; the harvester is to complete the work of the sower. The content and context of v. 36, then, indicate that Jesus is the harvester and God the sower.[104] The emphasis throughout the Fourth Gospel on Jesus' continuation and accomplishment of God's work (e.g., 5:36, 10:37-38, 14:10, 17:4) supports this interpretation of the metaphor of v. 36.

The specific narrative context of v. 36 also aids in interpreting the harvester metaphor. In the light of both vv. 30 and 35, Jesus' activity as harvester should be seen in relation to the approaching Samaritans. The Samaritans who will soon confess Jesus as savior (4:42) are the fruit of this particular harvest. Verse 36 can therefore be read both with general reference to the shared activity of Jesus and God and with specific reference to the Samaritan narrative.

Jesus expands the harvester/sower imagery through the introduction of a second proverb in v. 37: "For in this the saying is true, one sows and another harvests." This verse functions to hold vv. 35-38 together. The "for" *(gar)* with which the verse opens indicates that the proverb, "one sows and another reaps," is connected with what preceded it, but the proverb can also be understood as introducing a new topic which is then expanded in v.38. Verse 37 therefore has a transitional function in the series of harvest sayings;[105] it can be understood as a comment both on v. 36 and on v. 38. When v. 37 is read in connection with v. 36, the proverb's distinction between the harvester and the sower can be seen as balancing the unity of v. 36b. Even though the two rejoice at the same time, the sower and harvester remain two distinct persons. One can see a similar distinction in v. 34: Jesus completes the work of someone else, the one who sent him. When the proverb is read forward, it introduces the two distinct categories of v. 38, the "others" who labor and the disciples who harvest.[106] Verse 37 thus provides a way to move from the christological focus of v. 36 to the disciples in v. 38. The saying, "one sows and another reaps," envisions many analogous applications, as is the nature of proverbial speech, not one specific application.

Verse 37 therefore functions as a bridge from v. 36, in which Jesus is the harvester, to v. 38 in which the disciples assume that role. Verse 38 marks a decisive change in the harvest speech, for the disciples, who to this point have fulfilled the metaphorical role of observers of the harvest, are now thrust into the metaphorical role of active participants.[107] This change of role for the disciples is underscored by the change in temporal perspective. Jesus refers to his sending of the disciples as past, to the disciples' entrance into the others' labor as past ("I sent," "You did not labor," "others have labored," "you have entered"). These past tenses are difficult to interpret because the narrative provides no apparent context for them; they seem to indicate a shift away from the immediate story line.[108] The key to interpreting this verse and this entire section of Jesus' speech lies in clarifying its temporal perspective.

The temporal shift in v. 38 receives added significance when we remember that vv. 35–38 opened with a metaphorical affirmation of the arrival of the eschatological hour. Jesus' use of the harvest metaphor in vv. 35–38 thus presupposes a new understanding of time. The four-month waiting period between seedtime and harvest is no longer a valid way of measuring time. The coming of the hour changes the relationship between what is and what will be.

It is possible to explain the temporal shift of v. 38 as reflecting a post-resurrection perspective or a saying of the risen Jesus, along the lines of 20:21, "Just as the Father sent me, even so I send you." Yet simply reading v. 38 as post-resurrection is a distortion of what is at work both in the verse and in the Fourth Gospel in general. One cannot simply separate what is pre-resurrection/glorification from what is post-resurrection/glorification. Throughout the Gospel John presents both perspectives as constantly impinging on one another, as being simultaneously operative. In narrating the story of Jesus, John is not restricted by traditional chronology. John's unorthodox chronology can be seen clearly in John 3:13, "And no one has ascended into heaven except he who has descended from heaven, the Son of Man." In the Samaritan narrative, the knowledge that makes true worship possible, the worship in spirit and truth, is not presented as restricted to one point in Jesus' life, that is, post-glorification and after the sending of the Paraclete but is narrated as present *now* (4:23).

John therefore communicates a double vision of Jesus' life in which present and future impinge on one another. Verse 38 is a product of this vision, for it presents the future commissioning of the disciples as something which has already occurred (cf. "The hour is coming and now is," v. 23).[109] Verse 38 is not a transposed saying of the risen Jesus. Rather, it functions as the evangelist's interpretive comment on the harvest scene, couched within the narrative itself, in which he communicates the new relationship of past, present, and future evoked by the arrival of the hour/harvest.

The sequence of harvest sayings in vv. 35–38 offer the disciples instruction on Jesus' identity and function (vv. 36–37). In addition to its christological focus, the harvest imagery also serves to inform the disciples how and where they are called to stand in relation to Jesus' activity (vv. 35, 37, 38). In v. 33 the disciples ask questions about Jesus' food. The proverbs and metaphors of vv. 34–38, with their eschatological orientation, offer the disciples the answers to their questions.

Jesus' use of proverbs and metaphor in the scene with the disciples points to important differences between two-level language that is ironic and two-level language that is metaphorical. Jesus' use of *brōma* in v. 34 provides a bridge between irony and metaphor in this scene. The discussion of food begins ironically (vv. 31–33), but Jesus' own words in v. 34 are closer to metaphor. Jesus' figurative use of the harvest image is not primarily—often not at all—ironic. As previously mentioned, the disciples' misperception of the harvest and the Samaritans suggests an ironic context for the entire speech, but this irony is not a dominant thread as the sayings continue. The reader's relationship to the narrative therefore changes, because the metaphorical language of these verses does not invite the same series of choices and decisions as the ironic language does. Yet metaphor also invites reader participation, for the reader is still asked to see two meanings in a single image. These two meanings do not conflict, as in irony, but complement one another. Correct insight is still needed for the reader to move through the harvest imagery. Verses 7–26 have provided the reader with that insight. The ironic interplay of those verses drew the reader into the revelatory dynamic so that he or she was able to make the final decision to affirm or deny the *egō eimi* of v. 26; the process of vv. 31–38 presupposes and builds on that decision.

> (39) Many Samaritans from that city believed in him because of the woman's testimony, "He told me all that I ever did." (40) So when the Samaritans came to him, they asked him to stay with them; and he stayed there two days. (41) And many more believed because of his word. (42) They said to the woman, "It is no longer because of your words that we believe, for we have heard for ourselves, and we know that this is indeed the Savior of the world." (John 4:39–42)

John 4:39–42. In these verses the narrative focus returns to the Samaritans. As was the case earlier in the narrative, the conclusion of the scene with the disciples is marked by this reentry of the Samaritans. The Samaritans' actual arrival on the scene, however, is preceded by a reprise of vv. 29–30 in v. 39. The Samaritan woman's original words concerning Jesus are repeated, but important details are added which make v. 39 more than just a simple reprise. In vv. 29–30 the townspeople's response to the woman's words is not given. We may infer a positive reaction when they leave town and head for Jesus, but John does not specify their response. The portrait of the townspeople in v. 39 is quite different, for here John very explicitly describes their response: "Many Samaritans from that city believed in him because of the word of the woman who testified, 'He told me all that I ever did.' " This verse contains terms of special theological significance to John: believe *(pisteuō)*, word *(logos)*, testify *(martureō)*. It presents the woman in a very positive role: she is a witness who brings others to faith in Jesus. Yet as the precise verbal repetition of v. 29 in this verse shows, the witness which she gives to the townspeople is her own seemingly limited conception of Jesus' identity and function. The reader is momentarily left to ponder in which Jesus the Samaritans believe.

Verse 40 completes the action which the imperfect tense of v. 30 left open; the Samaritans arrive at the well.[110] As previously mentioned (p. 54), this encounter between Jesus and the Samaritans, as in the scenes with the Samaritan woman and the disciples, opens with a request, albeit one narrated indirectly ("they asked him to stay with them"). This request brings the narrative full circle. In v. 9 the Samaritan woman had balked at the idea of social interaction between Samaritans and Jews; here, as a result of the mediation of the Samaritan woman, the Samaritans are requesting that interaction.

For the first time in the narrative, a request is complied with: "and he was staying *(emeinen)* there two days" (au. trans.). Like the *edei* of v. 4, *menō* functions both in the story line and in the larger context of Johannine theology. "Dwelling" with Jesus has important theological implications in the Fourth Gospel, and it is not out of line to see those implications here. "To dwell" with Jesus is to have direct contact with him, to share in his relationship with God.[111] The note with which v. 40 concludes, therefore, is not just an incidental narrative detail but an important commentary on Jesus' relationship with the Samaritans.

Verses 41 and 42 support the view that Jesus' "dwelling" with the Samaritans means more than that he resided in their buildings for two days. These verses draw attention to two results of Jesus' dwelling with them. First, many more believed "on account of his word" *(logos)*. The contrast with the woman's word in v. 39 is obvious, since John uses the same phrase in reference to both the woman and Jesus. This verse does not discredit those who believed on account of the woman's word, however, because it focuses on the others who came to faith. The second result of dwelling with Jesus has a more complex relationship to the woman's earlier witness: "They said to the woman, 'It is no longer on account of your word *(lalian)* that we believe, for we ourselves have heard and know that this is truly the Savior of the world.' " The Samaritans no longer need to base their faith on the woman's word. This verse is slightly at odds with v. 41, since it seems to imply that the many more who come to believe through Jesus' word and the Samaritans who had earlier come to faith through the woman's word are speaking as one body with the same experience. This inconsistency can be explained by the exigencies of the narrative—John intends the confession of v. 42 to be the confession of all the Samaritans and therefore must bring both groups of believers together, but there seems to be more than this at issue here. John is emphasizing the one experience that both groups do share: the immediacy of the direct encounter of Jesus.[112]

Is there then a complete disparagement of the woman's words? That v. 42 speaks of the woman's word as *lalia* and v. 41 speaks of Jesus' word as *logos* could be seen as pointing in that direction,[113] but v. 39 makes a strict *lalia/logos* division impossible. In v. 39 the woman's testimony is also spoken of as *logos,* and John quite openly says that through it people came to faith. What is important to note is that the designation of the Samaritan woman's words as *lalia* occurs in a direct statement by the townspeople, whereas the designation of them as *logos* occurs in a comment by the evangelist. The Samaria narrative presents at least three different perceptions of what the woman says and does: her own, the townspeople's, and the evangelist's. The reader is therefore given the responsibility to unravel the tension among these views and judge the value of the woman's words.

The narrative context of the woman's words and activity is most determinative of their meaning and value. Verses 39–42, and v. 42 in particular, indicate a transcending or surpassing of the woman's word in favor of the direct expression of Jesus.[114] One can therefore see the woman's testimony, the ambiguous "He told me all that I ever did," on the same level as Jesus' request for water or the disciples' offer of food—words which initiate the process that leads to revelation. Verse 42 is not a simple rejection of the woman's words by the Samaritans but a recognition that they themselves have now experienced Jesus and his revelation.

The Samaria narrative comes to its conclusion with the Samaritans' confession of Jesus: "This is truly the Savior of the world" (v. 42). The wording of this confession has important points of contact with the preceding narrative. First, the woman's tentative confession of v. 29, "This couldn't be the Christ, could it?" is both affirmed and transcended by the Samaritans' confession. They offer a title that is not restricted to specific Messianic expectations (cf. v. 25).[115] Second, the relationship between salvation *(sōtēria)* in v. 22 and savior *(sōtēr)* in this verse cannot be overlooked. Each word occurs only once in the Fourth Gospel. In v. 22 Jesus' words stressed that *sōtēria* came from the Jews; John's use of *sōtēr* here underscores the Samaritans' acceptance of Jesus' offer of salvation. The irony that was suspected behind v. 22b is confirmed here: the salvation that originated from the Jews and that they rejected is readily accepted by non-Jews. Third, but closely related to these first two points, the designation of Jesus as the savior of the world has important thematic connections with the entire narrative. The Samaritans do not confess Jesus as a national savior. Jesus' identity has moved from that of a Jew to a universal savior.[116] In addition to showing that Jesus transcends national bounds, this confession also affirms the present reality of the eschatological hour. The hour in which the distinctions of "on this mountain" and "in Jerusalem" will disappear is indeed now.

Verses 39–42 thus form an appropriate conclusion to the Samaria narrative. Not only do they bring together important themes of the narrative, but they also provide the reader with a third treatment of the questions of Jesus' identity, function, and revelation, which have already been manifested in the scenes with the Samaritan woman and the disciples. These verses affirm in miniature what the reader has experienced through the whole Samaria narrative: one must participate in the revelatory dynamic in order to know who Jesus is.

CONCLUSION

Our analysis of John 4:4–42 has focused on the ways in which John's portrait of Jesus as revealer and his theology of revelation are reflected in his literary technique. John does not merely *present* the story of John 4 to the reader but instead narrates it in such a way that the reader *participates* in the narrative and the revelatory experience communicated by it. The reader encounters Jesus and his revelation, but, in contrast to Bultmann, he or she does so through the narrative itself. The narrative is therefore not expendable but is a central element of the revelatory experience.

John's principal means of engaging the reader in the narrative is through his use of irony. We have observed many different forms and uses of irony in John 4:4–42. The overall dramatic structure of the episode contributes to and develops some of the irony, for example, the dovetailing of scenes and the cross references, thematic, temporal, and spatial, from one scene to another. These structural interrelationships often indicate ironic contrasts and disparities. The reader is thus made aware that the narrative is not one-dimensional but multi-dimensional, with two contrasting narrative levels often occurring simultaneously. Another important ironic technique is John's frequent use of repetition. Throughout the Samaria narrative, the words of one character are picked up and repeated in the speech of another. The same expression is thereby given a new meaning in a new context. Through such repetitions the reader is asked to remember both the original usage and the new usage, a juxtaposition which highlights the ironic tension (e.g., "give me a drink" [v. 7]/"give me this water"[v. 15]).

We have noted other ironic techniques: the ironic contrast between what is anticipated and what is said (vv. 17 and 18), ironic questions based on misunderstanding or false assumptions and perceptions (vv. 12, 33), and the more general pattern of question and indirect response (vv. 9 and 10, vv. 12 and 13–14). Jesus' interlocutors themselves, the Samaritan woman and the disciples, also contribute to the irony of the narrative. Their responses to Jesus often indicate their blindness to the second level of the conversation, making the irony more apparent to the comprehending reader. The characters are therefore not presented as examples for the reader;[117] instead the narrative anticipates that the reader will do *more* or *other* than the characters, including the disciples, do.

Through these techniques and others that we have indicated in our analysis, John leads the reader into a relationship with the text and the Jesus contained within it. The key to understanding how irony functions in the Johannine theology of revelation is to grasp the type of reader participation that it presupposes. In order to read irony successfully, one must make the correct series of judgments and decisions, but this series is dependent on the prior recognition that there are decisions to be made. Irony does not *force* the reader to decide but *allows* the reader to become engaged. In irony the elements of demand and distance are held in a taut, highly charged balance. Irony allows the reader room for personal choice but at the same time anticipates and expects that the choice and decision will be made. The dialogue form of John 4:4–42 and the narrative in which it is embedded are excellent examples of this demand/distance tension. The dialogue allows the reader room to observe, to overhear the conversations between Jesus and his interlocutors,[118] but at the same time it provides the opportunity for the reader to become engaged directly in the narrative, to enter into the ironic interplay of the text.

As we noted above in our discussion of vv. 7–26, Jesus often does not provide the woman with the explicit information needed to interpret his words correctly and to understand his identity. Instead his implicit, often indirect, responses leave room for the woman's personal movement to Jesus. Yet as her unsuccessful attempts to communicate with Jesus indicate, if she wants to understand him, she *must* make this movement. The way irony functions in the text is a key to understanding how Jesus functions as revealer. This interdependency of *narrative mode* and *theological claim* points to the Fourth Gospel narrative as the locus of revelation. The connection between narrative mode and theological claim remains in effect when Jesus' language becomes more explicit. In vv. 34–38 Jesus speaks to his disciples, to those who have some inside knowledge about Jesus' identity. These verses presuppose the same state of awareness in the reader. Jesus' words in vv. 34–38 are truly explicit and comprehensible only if the correct series of judgments and decisions have been made in the first half of the dialogue. There is less irony in these verses because they build on the ironic engagement of the earlier verses. We therefore again see the text functioning for its readers the same way the hero does for his interlocutors.[119]

Our analysis of John 4:4–42 thus points to the inadequacies of language which does not take the narrative mode seriously in describing the Johannine theology of revelation. If we analyze Jesus' revelation in John 4 primarily on the basis of the *Was*, its content, then the Samaria narrative is at worst unnecessary and at best repetitive, since the prologue has already explicitly stated who and what Jesus is.[120] If we analyze the Samaria narrative primarily on the basis of the *Dass,* the sheer fact of Jesus, then the narrative as narrative is unnecessary. The *how* of the text, in particular the *how* of the revelatory irony, provides a more integrative approach to the study of Jesus and his revelation. As a result of John's use of irony to communicate the dynamics of revelation, the narrative does not mediate the revelation but *is* the revelation.

4

THE LOCUS OF REVELATION

Now Jesus did many other signs in the presence of the disciples, which are not written in this book; but these are written that you may believe that Jesus is the Christ, the Son of God, and that believing you may have life in his name. (John 20:30–31)

MODE AND CLAIM

These two verses form the conclusion to the main body of the Fourth Gospel.[1] Scholarly discussion of these two verses focuses primarily on what these verses say about the intended purpose of the Gospel, and in particular, on what audience is addressed by the "you may believe" of 20:31—believers or nonbelievers?[2] The debate over what particular type of believers the Fourth Evangelist had in mind should not, however, prevent us from grasping the two basic dimensions of this statement of purpose, dimensions that transcend all debate about audience. The first dimension of the Gospel's purpose is christological: "that you may believe that *Jesus is the Christ, the Son of God.*" The second is soteriological: "that believing *you may have life in his name.*" The community addressed by the Fourth Evangelist is one grounded in and empowered by the name and identity of Jesus.

What is particularly important about these two verses for our study of revelation in the Fourth Gospel, however, are the three verbs which lead up to the purpose clause in v. 31: "Jesus *did* many other signs . . . which *are not written* . . . but these *are* written. . . . " Verse

30 may draw attention to the "inexhaustible riches" of Jesus' activities, but the weight of the verbs of doing and writing does not rest there. Neither does the weight of these verbs rest in focusing attention on the selectivity of the evangelist in choosing among these riches.[3] The weight of these verbs, with their contrast between what *was* done and what *is* written, rests instead in their articulation of where the locus of revelation lies.

In v. 31, the purpose clause *(hina)* explicitly links "the things that are written" with the statements of christological and communal identity. The Fourth Evangelist does not say, "These things were *done* in order that you may believe." He says, "these things *are written* in order that you may believe."[4] The locus of revelation does not lie in the myriad of signs and deeds done by Jesus that are not recorded in the text, even if they were done in the presence of his disciples. Revelation does not lie in deeds that exist outside of the world of the Gospel because the deeds in and of themselves are not revelatory (cf. John 20:29).[5] Rather, the locus of revelation lies *in* the written narration of those things to which the reader of the Gospel is given access. By focusing on the written narration of Jesus' deeds, the Fourth Evangelist is asking us to take this narrative seriously. His words in these concluding verses explicitly draw our attention to the Gospel narrative as the locus of revelation.

This understanding of John 20:30–31 provides a helpful perspective from which to examine the different modes of revelation we discussed in chapter 2. For the Fourth Gospel, *narrative mode* and *theological claim* cannot be separated in any discussion of revelation. The Fourth Evangelist does not locate revelation in deeds, content, paradigms, dogma, or encounter that have an independent life outside of the Gospel text.[6] One cannot separate the fact of revelation or the content of revelation from the *mode* of revelation. John 20:30–31 brings us back to the notion of the "how" of revelation. *Revelation lies in the Gospel narrative and the world created by the words of that narrative!*

My analysis of John 4 has provided us with one example of the interplay in the Fourth Gospel between narrative mode and theological claim and demonstrated how the Fourth Gospel narrative functions as the locus of revelation. The Fourth Evangelist's use of irony enables the reader to participate in the Gospel narrative and to experience Jesus as revealer. For example, as noted, Jesus does not immediately reveal his identity to the Samaritan woman but instead invites her to discover it for herself (4:10). Through the Samaritan woman's ironic misunderstanding of both Jesus' identity and the proffered invitation (4:11, 12, 15), the reader is drawn into the narrative. Similarly, the reader is able to experience fully Jesus' *egō eimi* of 4:26 as a result of the ironic interplay of the preceding verses. The Fourth Evangelist does not simply present Jesus as revealer to his readers but constructs the Gospel text in such a way as to allow his readers to enter into the revelatory dynamic themselves.

The revelatory irony of John 4 makes it impossible to overlook the "how" of the revelatory dynamic of the Fourth Gospel narrative. The revelatory irony of John 4 does not present the reader with some content of revelation that she or he is asked to appropriate. Instead, the double exposure of irony simultaneously places two contradictory images or expressions before the reader without resolving the tension between them, and the reader is left to decipher the relationship between expression and meaning on his or her own. Neither, however, does the Fourth Evangelist's use of irony bring the reader to the bare fact of Jesus' presence. The "that" of revelation cannot be isolated from the narrative which gives the reader access to Jesus. Rather, it is in reading and interpreting irony, in the "how" of the revelatory dynamic, that the reader experiences Jesus as revealer.[7]

Johannine irony creates the revelation experience for the reader as a result of the imaginative participation in the text which it encourages.[8] The space that the indirectness of irony allows for the reader to move through the conflicting levels of meaning is the space for the imagination.

> What the language *says* is transcended by what it *uncovers,* and what it *uncovers* represents its true meaning. Thus the meaning of the literary work remains related to what the printed text says, but it requires the creative imagination of the reader to put it all together.[9]

What Wolfgang Iser says about the act of reading in general applies even more forcefully to the act of reading irony, because the indirectness of irony intensifies the role of the reader.[10]

John 4 provides many different ways for the reader to participate in the narrative. In 4:10 Jesus does not give a direct answer to the Samaritan woman's question of 4:9 ("How can you, a Jew . . . ") but leaves her with a question that asks her—and the reader—to reassess their perception of the situation. Similarly, the ironic distance between what the reader suspects and what the characters say draws the reader into the text. The irony of 4:33 arises because the reader is able to grasp that Jesus speaks of more than ordinary food while the disciples are not. The reader is drawn closer to Jesus as revealer through the disciples' misunderstanding.[11] The tension between what is said and what is meant, between what the reader anticipates and what the reader actually discovers, keep the reader constantly engaged with the text and, through the text, with Jesus as revealer. The demand/distance tension of irony allows the reader the room to interact with the text, to respond through his or her own experience of its images and expressions.

The role that irony creates for the imagination leads to the reader's participation in the text, to the series of judgments and decisions, interaction and response, that constitutes the interpretive process. Throughout the dialogue between Jesus and the Samaritan woman, the Fourth Evangelist allows two contradictory perceptions of the same event to stand side by side without comment. An explicit statement by Jesus (e.g., 4:23–24) is immediately undercut by the woman's response (4:25), and the reader is left to choose between the two alternatives. Through this participation the reader can then decide about what the text means, about its portrait of Jesus as revealer, and can decide whether to accept or reject his revelation.

The "how" of revelation in the Fourth Gospel, the invitation the Gospel narrative offers the reader to participate in the narrative and thus to experience how Jesus makes God known, is not restricted to the Fourth Evangelist's use of irony. Given the nature of irony, however, this "how" is most acutely present there. Throughout the Fourth Gospel, what is said cannot be experienced apart from how it is said! John 4 provides us with a detailed example of the Johannine revelatory mode. It will be helpful to complement this detailed analysis with examples of other places in the Fourth Gospel where the centrality of the "how" of revelation is visible.

The Bread of Life

(25) When they found him on the other side of the sea, they said to him, "Rabbi, when did you come here?" (26) Jesus answered them, "Truly, truly, I say to you, you seek me, not because you saw signs, but because you ate your fill of the loaves. (27) Do not labor for the food which perishes, but for the food which endures to eternal life, which the Son of man will give to you; for on him has God the Father set his seal." (28) Then they said to him, "What must we do, to be doing the work of God?" (29) Jesus answered them, "This is the work of God, that you believe in him whom he has sent." (30) So they said to him, "Then what sign do you do, that we may see, and believe you? What work do you perform? (31) Our fathers ate the manna in the wilderness; as it is written, 'He gave them bread from heaven to eat.' " (32) Jesus then said to them, "Truly, truly, I say to you, it was not Moses who gave you the bread from heaven; my Father gives you the true bread from heaven. (33) For the bread of God is that which comes down from heaven, and gives life to the world." (34) They said to him, "Lord, give us this bread always." (35) Jesus said to them, "I am the bread of life; he who comes to me shall not hunger, and he who believes in me shall never thirst." (John 6:25–35)

The revelatory language of John 6 and its portrait of Jesus as revealer have important points of contact with the language of John 4.[12] Like John 4, John 6 contains both narrative and dialogue, but unlike the interweaving of narrative and dialogue one finds in John 4, in John 6 the major dialogue (6:22–51) follows two narrative blocks (6:1–15; 16–21). Although narrative and dialogue can be more easily identified as distinct blocks of material in John 6, the two remain intimately connected in the "how" of the Johannine revelatory mode. The feeding of the five thousand (6:1–15) and Jesus' walking on water (6:16–21) establish the christological context out of which the dialogue emerges. Similarly, the lengthy dialogue that follows these two important narrative events provides a lens through which to interpret 6:1–21, an indication that the two acts in and of themselves are not the locus of revelation.

John 6:25–35 have the most immediate parallels with John 4. I will concentrate on these verses, which are part of a dialogue between Jesus and the crowd who had been fed in 6:1–15. This crowd has not been privy to Jesus' walking on the water. Only the disciples experienced that theophany. The crowd's ignorance of the theophany is underscored by their opening question to Jesus, "Rabbi, when did you come here?" The reader can correctly answer the crowd's question because the narrative has shown the reader both when and how Jesus "came here." As was frequently the case in John 4, the reader knows more than the crowd does. The reader's knowledge of Jesus' walking on the water provides the reader with a different access to the dialogue than that of the crowd. These different levels of knowledge are crucial in understanding the dialogue of John 6:25–35.

In my analysis of John 4 I noted that Jesus will frequently leave questions unanswered or answer them indirectly (4:9–10, 12–14). He does the same thing in this dialogue. Jesus does not tell the crowd when, or how, he arrived on the other side of the sea, but instead turns their question around to focus on why *they* have come to the other side of the sea. Jesus rebukes the crowd, and the formal language with which his response begins ("Truly, truly, I say to you . . .") underscores the seriousness of his rebuke. When Jesus has come across the sea, the narrative leads us to understand, is not what is important. What is important? The crowd's misplaced motivation for coming.

Jesus' rebuke of the crowd, "you seek me, not because you saw signs, but because you ate your fill of loaves," provides an explicit link between the feeding miracle of 6:1–15 and the dialogue. Jesus' words draw our attention back to the crowd's response to the feeding in 6:14 ("When the people saw the sign which he had done . . ."). The Fourth Evangelist has explicitly acknowledged that the crowd saw a sign, yet now Jesus' own words cast doubt on that acknowledgment. The boldness of Jesus' rebuke ("Truly, truly . . . ") brings the reader face to face with the question of what a sign *(semeia)* is and how one responds to it. According to Jesus' words in v. 26, the crowd cannot even see through the feeding to see a sign. They are motivated to seek Jesus solely because they ate their fill. This is not unlike the Samaritan woman, who wanted to receive Jesus' gift of living water so that she would no longer need to return to the well to draw drinking water.

In both John 4 and 6 Jesus and his interlocutors are conversing on two different levels. In John 6, by focusing on the difference between eating one's fill of bread and seeing a sign, Jesus indicates both the two levels of the feeding (and of the following dialogue) and the tension between the two levels. One cannot remain only on the first level, that is, be filled with bread, yet at the same time one cannot reject outright the literal level of the bread in pursuit of the "deeper" meaning. The two levels must be held in concert. We are confronted once again with the double exposure of irony. It is no accident that this revelatory dynamic of holding two contradictory images in concert occurs in a Gospel that has as its central affirmation, "The Word became flesh."

Jesus' words in 6:27 make the two levels of the conversation even more explicit. He establishes a contrast between labor for food that perishes *(apollumi)* and labor for food that remains *(menō)* to eternal life. This contrast, like Jesus' words in v. 26, establishes a verbal connection with the preceding feeding miracle ("Gather up the fragments left over, that nothing may be lost," *apollumi*). Jesus' words also anticipate the subject of the rest of the dialogue, the manna miracle (cf. Exod. 16:13–30, esp. vv. 18–21). This food that endures to eternal life, much like the living water in John 4, is a gift which the Son of man will give. At this point in the dialogue we have a traditional use of both food and gift: the subject, Son of man, and the object, food, of the verb "to give" are distinct. That traditional use will be radically transformed as the dialogue continues.[13]

The crowd's attention, however, is not focused on Jesus' words about food but on his words about work. The crowd responds to the verb "work" *(ergazomai)* but misunderstands Jesus' use of it. In v. 27 *ergazomai* implies "earn by working," "work for," but in v. 28 the crowd uses the same verb to mean "perform," "work a work."[14] Jesus and the crowd are using the same words to mean different things. Just as with the irony of John 4, their conversation is being simultaneously conducted on two distinct and conflicting levels. This becomes even clearer in Jesus' response in v. 29. First, Jesus replaces the crowd's expression, "the works of God," with the singular, "the work of God." Second, Jesus redefines work in terms of faith, "This is the work of God, that you believe in him whom God has sent."[15]

Jesus' response thus transforms the more traditional categories of the crowd, moving from works to one work. Jesus transforms the crowd's understanding of its work and God's work, redefining them in terms of his own identity and their response to his identity. This exchange between Jesus and the crowd is an important example of the movement and interplay that occur in this dialogue when the words of one party are picked up and reworked by the other conversation partner. The crowd's use of "work" here does not necessarily advance the dialogue in any traditional sense, because this dialogue does not always proceed according to our customary expectations of linear movement. The interplay in this dialogue is richer and more complex than any smooth progression from beginning to end, because getting to "the end" is not the goal of Johannine narratives such as this one. Rather, the way and the goal are frequently one. (This narrative dynamic corresponds to the Fourth Evangelist's understanding of who Jesus is: "I am the way, and the truth and the life" [14:6].) The verbal interplay in this narrative is crucial in experiencing how the Johannine Jesus makes God known.

The crowd's words in vv. 30–31 further indicate that this conversation is being conducted on two levels. The crowd's response shows that they connect Jesus' words in v. 29 about "the one sent" with Jesus himself and that they want to be able to do God's work, to believe. But their questions also ironically demonstrate their ignorance and lack of comprehension: "Then what signs do you do that we may see, and believe you? What work do you perform?" All the words of these questions ironically repeat key words from the dialogue: sign (v. 26), do (v. 28), see (v. 26), believe (v. 29), work (vv. 27, 28). An important shift has taken place, however, in the crowd's reworking of these terms. The burden of who is to work has shifted from the crowd (vv. 27–29) to Jesus (v. 30). Their words imply a contingency: they will do God's work only if Jesus does God's work first.

Yet the crowd's request for a sign and a work from Jesus is jarring in its narrative context. How can they make such a request immediately after the feeding miracle in which they have participated (6:14, 26)? This request for a sign is an important signal of the crowd's level of understanding and ironically proves Jesus' words of v. 26 to be correct. The crowd indeed does not seek Jesus because they saw a sign, for they are unable even to understand and interpret what they have experienced. They only know that they ate their fill. The demands of the crowd's questions, demands that have already been fulfilled before their eyes, accentuate the distance between the crowd and Jesus.

In John 4, the Samaritan woman compared Jesus with "our father Jacob" in an attempt to question Jesus' identity and to compare unfavorably his offer of water with Jacob's miraculous gift of water. The crowd makes a similar move here, although the explicit comparison is couched in terms of the fathers and the crowd. The comparison between Jesus and Moses is implicit. The stated contrast is between what was done for the fathers and what Jesus can do for them, that is, "we know what sign our fathers had; what sign will we have?" The fact that the crowd, like the fathers, has been fed with miraculous bread makes the irony of this contrast unavoidable. Perhaps to give added weight to their reference to their forebears, the feeding with manna in the wilderness is recounted through a quotation from Scripture. The Word of God is called on to do battle over what is the work of God.

This quotation from Scripture (cf. Ps. 78:24; Exod. 16:4, 15) provides the basis for the remainder of Jesus' remarks to the crowd in this section of the dialogue. It is possible to interpret Jesus' reworking of the quotation as an example of midrashic technique.[16] It is important to keep in mind, however, that we have seen the reuse and transformation of one character's words in the mouth of another as a consistent element of Johannine narrative style, not limited to the interpretation of Scripture.

Jesus reworks four elements of the crowd's quotation of scripture:
1. not Moses . . . my Father
2. gave . . . gives
3. bread from heaven . . . true bread from heaven
4. to you (the fathers) . . . to you (the crowd)[17]

The identity of the donor of the bread is reinterpreted, as is the time of the gift, the nature of the gift, and the recipients of the gift. The gift of the past with which the crowd is concerned is superseded by the gift of the present. Jesus' reworking of this quotation answers the crowd's demands of 6:30, although they do not recognize this. To the reader of the Gospel, the contrasts of this verse recall the words of the prologue, "For the law was given through Moses; grace and truth came through Jesus Christ" (1:17). The reader has a context for understanding these words of Jesus that is not available to the crowd.

Jesus expands on the meaning of "true bread from heaven" in 6:33 and, as he does so, continues to transform the crowd's categories. The true bread of heaven is now spoken of as the bread of God, and that bread is described with two predicates: (1) that which comes down from heaven and (2) that which gives life to the world. For the reader of the Gospel, but not for the crowd, these two expressions will both sound familiar and will resonate with what has already been said about Jesus in the Fourth Gospel. In 3:13, the language of ascent and descent was used in reference to the Son of man: "No one has ascended into heaven but he who descended from heaven, the Son of man."[18] In 5:21, the Fourth Gospel affirms that it is Jesus who gives life to the world: "for as the Father raises the dead and gives them life, so also the Son gives life to whom he will" (cf. 5:25–26).

We see therefore that these descriptions of the bread of God in 6:33 will lead the reader to anticipate and perhaps to recognize that this dialogue is not merely about the multiplication miracle, but it is also about Jesus. As a result of having read the Gospel, the reader can grasp that this is now a christological dialogue. The tension between what the reader knows and what the crowd knows, between the two different understandings of what it means to speak of the bread that comes down from heaven and gives life, contains an anticipatory irony for the reader as she or he awaits the crowd's response to these words of Jesus.

This anticipatory irony becomes full irony in 6:34. The crowd's request in v. 34, "Sir, give us this bread always," reveals that they see neither that Jesus is speaking about anything other than bread nor what type of bread is being discussed. The similarity between this request for bread and the Samaritan woman's request for water in 4:15 is unmistakable and universally recognized.[19] Like the Samaritan woman, the crowd of John 6 has understood one part of Jesus' words, that the bread of which he speaks is better than the bread given to their fathers, but does not grasp why it is better. The adverb "always" provides an important clue to their level of misunderstanding and drives home the irony of their request. The bread of which Jesus speaks is not given always, but need be given only once.

In the face of such ironic misunderstanding, Jesus reveals himself directly, "I am the bread of life; the one who comes to me shall not hunger, and the one who believes in me shall never thirst" (6:35). The contrast between this bold statement and the crowd's request is powerful and evocative. In our analysis of John 4, we noted that the *egō eimi* of 4:26 was effective as revelatory discourse because of the participatory nature of the narrative that precedes it. The same narrative dynamic is operative here. Jesus' self-revelation in 6:35 addresses and resolves the crowd's misunderstanding, but it also reinforces the irony of their remarks in the process. For example, the crowd has requested a continuous supply of bread ("always," *pantote*), but Jesus proclaims that those who come to him will not hunger and will never *(ou mē . . . pōpote)* thirst. In other words, if the crowd understood Jesus correctly, it would know that a continuous supply of the true bread of heaven would be superfluous (cf. 4:13–14).

The *egō eimi* of 6:35 confirms the reader's expectation that the description of the bread in v. 33 should be linked with Jesus. Yet this *egō eimi* intensifies the irony of the crowd's ignorance at the same time as it confirms the reader's knowledge. The bread the crowd requested is already before them and in fact is the very person of whom they are making the request. Jesus is the bread of life and his presence answers all their demands, but the crowd does not know what it sees (6:30, 36) and therefore cannot make this crucial connection.

The revelation of this text from John 6 cannot finally be located in the words, "I am the bread of life" in isolation, because those words have no real meaning apart from the narrative context in which they are embedded. Those words are able to communicate and evoke the reality of Jesus' identity and presence to the reader only because the reader has moved through the Gospel narrative. Neither can the revelation finally be located in the miraculous act of feeding five thousand people or in Jesus' walking on the water, because these two acts, like the dialogue which follows, cannot be isolated from their narrative context and presentation. What we discover when we read this section of John 6 is that the narrative dynamic of this text invites and enables the reader to participate in the narrative and thus to experience for himself or herself the way in which Jesus makes God known in the Fourth Gospel. This section from John 6, with its imaginative combination of irony, misunderstanding, and word play, makes clear, as John 4 does as well, that God's revelation in Jesus cannot be identified simply as propositions or as deeds or as subjective encounter, because to do so nullifies the revelatory power of the Fourth Gospel text. We will only fully answer the question, "How is God made known in the Fourth Gospel?" when we allow the "how" of revelation, the narrative dynamics of the Fourth Gospel text, to be an equal partner in the conversation.

THE FAREWELL DISCOURSE

(25) I have said this to you in figures; the hour is coming when I shall no longer speak to you in figures but tell you plainly of the Father. (26) In that day you will ask in my name; and I do not say to you that I shall pray the Father for you; (27) for the Father himself loves you, because you have loved me and have believed that I came from the Father. (28) I came from the Father and have come into the world; again, I am leaving the world and going to the Father. (29) His disciples said, "Ah, now you are speaking plainly, not in any figure! (30) Now we know that you know all things, and need none to question you; by this we believe that you came from God." (31) Jesus answered them, "Do you now believe? (32) The hour is coming, indeed it has come, when you will be scattered, every man to his home, and will leave me alone; yet I am not alone, for the Father is with me. (33) I have said this to you, that in me you may have peace. In the world you have tribulation; but be of good cheer, I have overcome the world." (John 16:25–33)

The "how" of revelation comes to our attention in a different way in the farewell discourse. As we noted earlier in the introduction, the mode of Jesus' revelation is given explicit mention in 16:25–33. John 16:25 is the hinge on which the rest of the pericope depends: "These things I have said to you *in figures (en paroimiais);* the hour is coming when I shall no longer speak to you *in figures (en paroimiais)* but will tell you *plainly (parresią)* about the Father." Jesus' words here explicitly focus the disciples' (and the reader's) attention on the ways in which Jesus makes God known. Jesus mentions two modes of revelatory speech: speech that is in figures and speech that is plain. How are we to understand the relationship between these two revelatory modes? And how do these modes help us to understand the revelatory dynamic of the Fourth Gospel?

In order to answer these questions, it is important to clarify how the expressions "in figures" *(en paroimiais)* and "plainly" *(parresia̧)* are used in 16:25. First, it is widely accepted that the figurative language to which the expression *en paroimiais* refers is not restricted to the immediately preceding words of Jesus (the figure of the woman in labor),[20] nor just to the words of the farewell discourse. The reference to speaking in figures is understood to include all of Jesus' teaching.[21] Second, the expression is not used to refer to isolated units of Jesus' teaching, to one proverb or parable, but it is used adverbially to describe Jesus' mode of communicating.[22] Finally, the meaning of *en paroimiais* can only be understood in the context of its relationship with *parresia̧* and vice versa.[23] In the Fourth Gospel, *parresia̧* is used to indicate Jesus' public words and deeds (7:26, 11:54) and the openness with which Jesus makes many of his claims (10:24–25, 18:20). We can therefore define "speak openly" as "announce in a way that makes manifest," and, as its opposite, define "speak in figures" as "speak in a way that conceals."[24]

The traditional interpretation of 16:25 is that the time of Jesus' revelation in figures is his earthly ministry, and that this revelation will be succeeded by the open revelation in the time after the resurrection. The contrast between the past and future tense of the verbs in 16:25 and the expression "the hour is coming" are taken to imply that Jesus revealed indirectly in the past and will reveal openly only in the future. All of Jesus' speech during his ministry is therefore cryptic, and full revelation is possible only in the future.[25]

Does John 16:25, however, establish this strict chronological relationship between revelation *en paroimiais* and revelation *parresia̧,* or does it point to an understanding of Jesus' revelatory mode that is richer and more complex than such a chronological resolution would allow? The way one answers this question is crucial for understanding the function of Johannine revelatory language and the type of participation made possible by such language.

The immediate context of 16:25, 16:25–33, calls the traditional two-stage interpretation of 16:25 into question, because the pericope reveals that 16:25 is not a straightforward statement to be taken at face value but is itself ironic.[26] Jesus is challenging his disciples to move through the ironic incongruities of his literal statement to his intended meaning. The disciples' response to Jesus' words shows that they did not perceive Jesus' challenge and therefore did not move with him.

In their response in 16:29, the disciples intend to confirm Jesus' statement of 16:25 but instead demonstrate that they have not understood his words: "Ah, now you are speaking plainly *(en parresią)*, not in any figure *(paroimian)."* At first glance the disciples' words appear to be an example of simple misunderstanding: Jesus spoke of the future revelation that would be open and the disciples wrongly apply these words to the present. But the relationship between open and figurative revelation, between direct and indirect speech, is not simply a matter of chronological location. The tension and distance between Jesus' words in 16:25–28 and the disciples' response in 16:29–30 is more far-reaching than a confusion of present and future time.

The distance between the two is highlighted by the verbal repetition of 16:25 in 16:29, a pattern we have noted also in John 4 and 6. This repetition juxtaposes the original usage of *en paroimiais/parresią* with its new usage by the disciples. Jesus spoke of "figures" in the plural, the disciples speak of "figure" in the singular. This change from plural to singular indicates that the disciples do not understand that Jesus is referring to his mode of speaking, but instead interpret his words as if Jesus were referring to individual teaching units. The disciples' response shows that they do not understand that Jesus is speaking of the "how" of revelation, and they thereby restrict the scope and application of Jesus' words.

The disciples assert their interpretation of Jesus' words and their knowledge in such bold language that the distance between them and Jesus becomes even more difficult to ignore. In 16:29 they say, *"Ah, now* you are speaking plainly" and in 16:30, *"Now we know* that you know everything . . . by this we believe that you came from God." Their confidently asserted knowledge, their bold assumption that *now* they know and believe opens itself to close scrutiny. Their words ironically indicate their true level of understanding, which is almost no understanding at all (cf. 4:15, 29; 6:34).

The disciples' remarks conclude with their affirmation that "in this we believe that you have come from God." Bultmann notes that the disciples acknowledge Jesus' words in 16:28 about his origin, "I came from the Father and have come into the world" but ignore the complementary expression that completes Jesus' relationship to God, "Again I leave the world and go to the Father."[27] This omission further undercuts the disciples' confident confession, "Now we know . . . and believe."[28] In Jesus' words in 16:25–28 and in the disciples' response in 16:29–30, a connection is made between *how Jesus speaks* and *how he makes God known.*

Jesus' words in John 16:31, "Now you believe,"[29] ironically echo the disciples' confession in vv. 29–30[30] and cast doubt on what they do indeed know and believe. The emphatic use of "now" by Jesus *(arti)* parodies the disciples' emphatic use of "now" *(nun,* vv. 29, 30), and Jesus' repetition of "believe" explicitly challenges the disciples' statement of faith. Again we see the reworking of one character's words in the words of the other conversation partner, a narrative technique that frequently emphasizes distance and misunderstanding. There can be no doubt that the disciples have misinterpreted Jesus' words.

In John 16:32 Jesus points to the consequences of the disciples' misperception: "Behold the hour is coming and now has come when you will be scattered, each to his own home, and you will leave me alone." This saying of Jesus points in two directions. It affirms the necessity of the disciples' participation in the suffering of the hour (cf. 16:33) but denounces their loss of loyalty in the face of that suffering. The disciples do not grasp the connection between their confession and the hour, much as the Samaritan woman could not grasp the significance of the eschatological hour. Their abandonment of Jesus further underscores their misperception of his relationship to God, because even though the disciples abandon him, he will not be alone ("Yet I am not alone, for the Father is with me"). The disciples' confident confession of what they know pales dramatically in the face of the reality known and recounted by Jesus.

It is important to note that in his response to the disciples, Jesus transforms his own temporal categories. In 16:25 the hour in which Jesus will no longer speak in figures is still coming, but in 16:32 the hour has come. At first glance, therefore, it appears that Jesus confirms the disciples' application of his words to the present, but a closer reading reveals that Jesus exposes the inadequacy of the disciples' interpretation in a more profound way than the reader had at first suspected. The disciples' "now" speaks of the ordinary present, but Jesus speaks of the eschatological present. A similar contrast between the ordinary present and the eschatological present is also at the heart of 4:21–24. John 16:33 makes this transformation of times clear: "But be of good cheer, I have conquered *(nenikēka)* the world." The present now stands transformed by Jesus' *victory* over the world, but there is no access to this transformation without Jesus. The disciples' real mistake was in not recognizing the new relationship among past, present, and future which Jesus' presence inaugurates. All of the disciples' assumptions and presuppositions must be transformed by Jesus' ultimate victory over the world. Until the disciples submit to that victory and the resultant transformation of *all* categories, the distance between Jesus and his disciples remains.

Once again we find the interplay of a Johannine dialogue culminating in a direct statement of Jesus' identity (cf. 4:26, 6:35), in this case Jesus as the one who has conquered the world. Yet again, as in John 4 and 6, this direct statement has revelatory power only because it is firmly embedded in its narrative context, a context characterized by irony, word play, and misunderstanding. The revelation of this text cannot be located in the statement of 16:33 in and of itself.

What is most striking about 16:25–33 is that in this pericope the Fourth Evangelist provides us with explicit pointers to the revelatory dynamic that is playing itself out in the dialogue. When the Johannine Jesus speaks of revelation *en paroimiais* and revelation *parresią*, he gives a name to the revelatory dynamic that has been inherently present throughout the Gospel narrative. The two revelatory modes mentioned in 16:25 are not related to one another in a linear progression but are simultaneously operative in Jesus' revelation. In my analysis of John 4 and 6, I have pointed to the interplay between open and veiled revelation, between direct and indirect speech. I have also suggested that the correct interpretation of this interplay is not to reject one mode in favor of the other but to allow the two modes to be present together in the narrative. The revelatory dynamic of the Fourth Gospel rests in the interplay between revelation *en paroimiais* and revelation *parresiạ,* and in the transformation of categories and assumptions that takes place through the juxtaposition of those two modes.

CONCLUSION

When we think about the "how" of revelation in the Fourth Gospel, we are finally brought, as the Gospel narrative itself is, to the cross. The cross, this particular and decisive way that Jesus makes God known, confronts us in ways that make all former assumptions and categories obsolete. This is true throughout the New Testament (see the classic statement in 1 Cor. 1:18–25) but is perhaps nowhere more acutely obvious than in the Johannine narrative treatments of Jesus' passion.

At three points in the Fourth Gospel Jesus predicts his passion. He does not use the traditional language of the Synoptic passion predictions (cf. Mark 8:31; 9:31; 10:33–34 and parallels) but instead speaks of being "lifted up" (3:14; 8:28; 12:32).[1] This verb, "to lift up" *(hupsoō)*, like many words we have examined in this study of John 4 and 6, has a double meaning. *Hupsoō* means both "to lift up" and "to raise high," in the physical sense of lifting as well as "to exalt."[2] The Fourth Evangelist quite intentionally speaks of the cross with this word so that the reader can see that just as physical lifting up and exaltation are superimposed in the meaning of the verb *(hupsoō)*, so too are they superimposed in the event of the cross. The lifting up is incomplete without the accompanying exaltation, but similarly, and perhaps most importantly, there is no exaltation unless there is the physical lifting up on the cross. The words the Fourth Evangelist uses to speak about the cross are essential to what he wants to

communicate about the cross. What we have, then, in these Johannine predictions of Jesus' passion is another example of the insepara-
bility of *narrative mode* and *theological claim.* The "how" of the Fourth
Evangelist's words about the cross confront us with the "how" of the
cross itself.

In the trial before Pilate, the "how" of the narrative also brings us
to the "how" of the cross. John 18:28—19:16 is a masterpiece of
Johannine narrative technique, and the central role of irony in this
text has been noted.[3] Here I simply want to make a few suggestive
remarks in line with our discussion of revelation.

This trial scene differs markedly from those in the Synoptic Gospels, most noticeably in terms of its length and the amount of dialogue between Jesus and Pilate. As we should expect from the Fourth
Evangelist, he does not simply report the trial to his readers but
narrates it in such a way that the reader participates in the revelation
experience. In this trial, Pilate attempts to exercise his power and
authority over Jesus, but what the reader senses from the workings
of the narrative is that Pilate never achieves mastery. Instead, Pilate's
power and authority diminish as the narrative progresses. His questions and responses to Jesus underscore his distance from any true
command of power, authority, and knowledge. Yet the Fourth Evangelist does not *tell* the reader that Pilate is ineffectual, that Pilate is
powerless and without authority. Instead he allows the narrative to
draw the reader in so that the reader can form his or her own conclusions.

What the narrative shows the reader is a ruler with all the ac-
coutrements of power, with the authority to take away life, who
stands powerless in the face of true power, authority, and life. Pilate's
frenetic movement inside and outside of the praetorium during the
trial embodies his ineffectualness. The trial narrative does what the
cross does, it calls into question all the accepted categories of power,
of death, and of truth.[4] Pilate's question, "What is truth?" is not a
question that can be answered by categories of dogma, encounter, or
propositions that exist independently of this Gospel narrative. Jesus
has already answered the question of truth, and the reader of the
Gospel knows this (14:6). The locus of revealed truth lies in Jesus, a
Jesus the Fourth Gospel has been at pains to make available to the

reader. Like the crowd of 6:25–35, Pilate does not know the "truth" when he is looking at "him." Again narrative mode and theological claim are inseparable as the Gospel narrative brings the reader face to face with Jesus at his "hour."

My reading of the Fourth Gospel has shown that revelation, the "making known of God," cannot be subsumed under rubrics such as those we discussed in chapter 2: content, paradigm, encounter, dogma. Rather, revelation in the Fourth Gospel is available in ways that transform all such rubrics. What Amos Wilder writes about the error of attempting to reduce the kerygma to existential categories can be applied to similar approaches to revelation in the Fourth Gospel:

> The kerygma in itself as address and encounter is abstract and disembodied. It is supposed to represent God's grace and demand, engaging our freedom. But this is to reduce the mystery of revelation to the category of the will. The transactions between men and gods are richer than that.

Wilder goes on to say that it is only through a total register of images, metaphors, and stories "that the Gospel can reenact itself anew in any time."[5]

It is the Fourth Evangelist's freedom in making use of such a "total register" of narrative possibilities that gives the Fourth Gospel its richness and power. The Fourth Gospel's narrative makes available to the reader an experience of Jesus and the God known in Jesus in ways that resist our attempts to assimilate them into systematic categories. We will not "behold his glory, glory as of the only Son from the Father" (1:14) until we allow the Fourth Gospel's narrative embodiment of Jesus to have its full say. The Word does indeed dwell among us, but our analysis of the "how" of the Johannine revelatory dynamic shows that it is not the Word alone, but words, language as creation and expression, that bring the reader to the revelation of Jesus through imaginative participation in the text.

Our yearning for revelation is not adequately answered by affirmations that claim that the locus of revelation lies in the message of the text, the events behind the text, the person behind the text, or the proclamation in front of the text. Such affirmations restrict the arena in which God is made known because they overlook the intrinsic relationship of narrative mode and theological claim. The revelatory word can have full access to us only when we affirm that the locus of revelation lies in the Gospel text and in the world created by the words of that text. The Fourth Gospel answers our yearning for revelation by inviting the reader to enter that world and to be addressed by the life-giving disclosure from God in the text.

NOTES

INTRODUCTION

1. Both Hans Frei, *The Eclipse of Biblical Narrative* (New Haven: Yale Univ. Press, 1975) and Ronald Thiemann, *Revelation and Theology: The Gospel as Narrated Promise* (Notre Dame, Ind.: Univ. of Notre Dame Press, 1985) are recent theologians who deal explicitly with the relationship between revelation and the authority and character of Scripture. Both books make crucial contributions to the study of narrative and revelation. Both scholars emphasize the centrality of biblical narrative in their discussions of revelation, but the categories with which both finally operate and through which they see the text are categories of doctrine.

2. For a discussion of these Old Testament texts in relation to the question of presence, see Samuel Terrien, *The Elusive Presence: Toward a New Biblical Theology* (New York: Harper & Row, 1978).

3. As cited in Wilhelm Büchner, "Über den Begriff der Eironeia," *Hermes: Zeitschrift für klassische Philologie-Einzelschriften* 4 (1941):358.

4. See R. Alan Culpepper's work on Johannine irony in *Anatomy of the Fourth Gospel: A Study in Literary Design* (Philadelphia: Fortress Press, 1983), chap. 6; and Paul Duke's work on irony in *Irony in the Fourth Gospel* (Atlanta: John Knox Press, 1985). Duke's book is the published version of his dissertation, which he wrote under Culpepper's direction.

5. I have chosen to discuss only the most recent and significant studies of Johannine irony in this introduction, but the works of three other scholars deserve mention in the notes. The earliest explicit attempt to analyze Johannine irony was a paper presented by H. Clavier at the International Congress on "The Four Gospels in 1957" (*Studia Evangelica* 1 [1959]: 261–76). Clavier is not interested in irony for the insights it can give to the dynamics of the

Gospel of John, but for the insights it can give to the question of the historical Jesus. Clavier does not bring us to an understanding of the distinctly Johannine use of irony and its relation to Johannine theology. Jakob Jonsson's *Humor and Irony in the New Testament. Illustrated by Parallels in Talmud and Midrash* (Reykjavik: Bokautgafa Menningarsjods, 1965) is heavily influenced by Clavier in his understanding of and approach to irony, but he reduces Clavier's insights to a facile and superficial level. Jonsson provides a quite uncritical survey of New Testament texts that he recognizes as humorous or ironical, terms which he does not clearly differentiate. His treatment of Johannine irony is quite unsatisfactory. Finally, David W. Wead offers an analysis of Johannine irony in "The Literary Devices in John's Gospel" (Theol. Diss. 4; Basel: Kommissionverlag F. Reinhardt, 1970), chap. 4. See also, idem, "Johannine Irony as a Key to the Author-Audience Relationship in John's Gospel," *American Academy of Religion, Biblical Literature: 1974,* comp. by Fred O. Francis (Missoula, Mont.: Scholars Press, 1974), 33–50. Wead follows the model of Sophoclean tragedy and the dramatic irony associated with it (for a discussion of this understanding of irony, see my chap. 1) in his analysis of Johannine irony. Wead's analysis contains a helpful identification of themes that John develops ironically (*Literary Devices,* 55–67), but falls short because of his circumscribed understanding of irony.

6. Culpepper, *Anatomy of the Fourth Gospel,* 169–75.

7. Duke, *Irony in the Fourth Gospel,* 92.

8. Ibid., 151–55.

9. Ibid., 153.

10. Culpepper, *Anatomy of the Fourth Gospel,* 180. Culpepper goes so far as to say that "Never is the reader the victim of irony" (p. 179).

11. Ibid., 179.

12. Duke, *Irony in the Fourth Gospel,* 53.

13. George W. MacRae, S. J., "Theology and Irony in the Fourth Gospel," in *The Word in the World, Essays in Honor of F. L. Moriarty,* ed. R. J. Clifford and G. W. MacRae (Cambridge, Mass.: Weston College Press, 1973), 83–96.

14. Ibid., 83.

15. Ibid., 84.

16. Ibid., 87.

17. Ibid., 88.

18. In chap. 1 of this book we shall see that the presupposition of common knowledge is a prerequisite of all successful irony, not just dramatic irony, but the observation is still correct—John's use of irony presupposes a comprehending community. Unlike Wead, MacRae's analysis of Johannine irony as dramatic irony is not trapped by a view of superior knowledge drawn from Sophocles but inquires perceptively into the uniquely Johannine aspects of this knowledge.

19. MacRae, "Theology and Irony," 89.

NOTES

20. Ibid., 94.

21. See, esp., Herbert Schneider, "The Word Was Made Flesh: An Analysis of the Theology of Revelation in the Fourth Gospel," *CBQ* 31 (1969): 344–56.

22. Rudolf Bultmann, *The Gospel of John* (Philadelphia: Westminster Press, 1971), 63.

23. See my discussion of John 4:21–24 in my chap. 3.

24. Both scholars correctly draw attention to the relationship between Johannine dualism and irony, focusing in particular on the spatial aspects of this dualism (e.g., earth/heaven, below/above). (Culpepper, *Anatomy of the Fourth Gospel*, 167; Duke, *Irony in the Fourth Gospel*, 146–7).

25. Neil Schaeffer, "Irony," *The Centennial Review* 19 (1975):182.

26. Oscar Cullman, "Der johanneische Gebrauch doppeldeutiger Ausdrücke als Schlüssel zum Verständnis des vierten Evangeliums," *TZ* 4 (1948): 360–72. See the discussion of this article by David M. Granskou in "Structure and Theology in the Fourth Gospel: A Study of Literary Features in the Fourth Gospel and Their Relation to its Theology" (Ph.D. diss., Princeton Theological Seminary, 1960), 208.

27. J. Louis Martyn, *History and Theology in the Fourth Gospel*, 2d ed. (Nashville: Abingdon Press, 1979), 37. Italics mine.

28. Bultmann, *The Gospel of John*, 63.

29. Wayne C. Booth, *A Rhetoric of Irony* (Chicago: Univ. of Chicago Press, 1974), esp. 11–12. For a full discussion of this aspect of irony, see my chap. 1.

30. Bultmann, *The Gospel of John*, 341.

31. See the discussion of Quintilian in my chap. 1, pp. 16–18, 28.

32. William A. Beardslee, "Plutarch's Use of Proverbial Forms of Speech," *Semeia* 17 (1980): 101–12, esp. 109.

33. For my fuller discussion of 16:25–33, see chap. 4.

CHAPTER 1. THE ESSENCE AND
FUNCTION OF IRONY

1. Examples of the widespread contemporary usage of the word "irony" can be found in discussions of almost any subject matter. "Irony" occurs with particular frequency in news and sports reporting. A representative example is found in this sentence from Donald E. Hall, *Fathers Playing Catch with Sons* (San Francisco: North Point Press, 1985), 50: "While George Brett climbs the glorious mountain of his prime, all gut and muscle, his brother Ken watches with admiration and irony from the shadows of his quick sundown. . . . "

2. The noun *eirōn* first appears in *The Clouds* 449, the noun *eirōneia* in the *Republic* 337a. Two important discussions of classical irony are found in G. G. Sedgewick, *Of Irony, Especially in Drama* (Toronto: Univ. of Toronto Press, 1948) and Ernst Behler, *Klassische Ironie, Romantische Ironie, Tragische Ironie; Zum*

Ursprung Dieser Begriffe (Darmstadt: Wissenschaftliche Buchgellschaft, 1972). Our discussion of the concept "irony" covers much of the same material but does so with different organizational principles and thematic concerns.

3. In addition to *The Clouds,* see also *The Wasps* 174 and *The Birds* 1211.

4. *Symposium* 216de, 218d, *Euthydemus* 302b.

5. *Republic* 337a.

6. R. Alan Culpepper (*Anatomy of the Fourth Gospel,* 180) explicitly contrasts Socratic and Johannine irony.

7. For an example of *eironeia* as pure abuse, see Demosthenes, *First Phillippic* 7, a work contemporaneous with Plato's dialogues.

8. *Nicomachean Ethics* 4.7.14–17 (Ostwald translation).

9. *Art of Rhetoric* 2.5.11–12.

10. *Art of Rhetoric* 2.2.24–25.

11. *Art of Rhetoric* 3.18.7.

12. *Rhetoric to Alexander* 1434^a.17 ff.

13. *Characters* Preface 2–4.

14. Behler, *Klassische Ironie,* 21–23.

15. *Characters* 1.

16. *De Oratore* 2.65.261, 2.67.269.

17. *De Officus* 1.29.103–104. Cicero eliminates Aristotle's criterion of personal gain from his argumentation. The reason for this is clear—Cicero is principally interested in irony as a means of personal gain, in its efficacy as a tool for winning arguments (*De Oratore* 3.53.203).

18. *De Oratore* 2.67.272.

19. See the discussion of Norman Knox, *The Word Irony and its Context, 1500–1755* (Durham, N.C.: Duke Univ. Press, 1961), 45–75, 99ff. The most accomplished example of this technique is probably *A Modest Proposal* by Jonathan Swift, in which Swift "advocates" child cannibalism as a solution to Ireland's economic problems. Quintilian discusses blame-by-praise in *Institutio* 8.6.51 and adds its inverse, praise-by-blame.

20. *De Oratore* 2.67.269.

21. *Academica* 2.74.

22. *De Oratore* 2.67.270–271, *Academica* 2.15, *Brutus* 85.292. It is important to note, however, that Cicero did place some restrictions on the use of irony— he found it inappropriate for friendship, criminal testimony, and business transactions (e.g., *De Officus* 3.60–61).

23. August Haury, *L'Ironie et L'Humor chez Ciceron* (Leiden: E. J. Brill, 1955), 21.

24. For example, *Institutio* 4.1.38–39, 4.1.70, 8.6.55–56.

25. *Institutio* 1.Pr.9.

26. *Institutio* 4.1.38–39.

27. *Institutio* 6.2.15–16.

28. *Institutio* 8.6.1.

29. *Institutio* 9.1.4.

30. *Institutio* 9.1.14.

31. *Institutio* 8.6.2.

32. *Institutio* 8.6.40.

33. *Institutio* 8.6.54.

34. *Institutio* 8.6.54–55.

35. Cf. Wayne C. Booth, *A Rhetoric of Irony* (Chicago: Univ. of Chicago Press, 1974), 10–11: "In fact the distinction between internal and external or extrinsic clues—relied on so heavily in much modern criticism—becomes strangely irrelevant when one is deciding whether a passage is ironic."

36. To Quintilian's second point, cf. D. C. Muecke, *The Compass of Irony* (London: Methuen & Co., Ltd., 1969), 29: "The first formal requirements of irony are that there should be a confrontation or juxtaposition of contradictory, incongruous, or otherwise incompatible elements. . . . But we need more than this—we also need ironic intention." To Quintilian's third point, cf. the following quotation from Jonathan Culler cited in Frederic V. Bogel, "Irony, Inference, and Critical Uncertainty," *Yale Review* n.s. 69 (1979/80):11: "For a sentence to be properly ironic it must be possible to imagine some group of readers taking it quite literally. Otherwise there is no contrast between apparent and assumed meaning and no space of ironic play." Bogel's whole article focuses on this point.

37. For a general discussion of the effects of figures on meaning, see *Institutio* 9.1.10–11.18.

38. *Institutio* 9.2.45–47. For a discussion of the relationship of metaphor, allegory, and irony, see pp. 87–90.

39. Booth, *Rhetoric of Irony*, 139.

40. Ibid.

41. *Institutio* 9.1.7. See also 9.1.3.

42. Cicero attributed much of the irony of the Platonic dialogues to the "irony of the other master [Socrates], especially as it was unending" (*Academica* 2.74).

43. "Field of observation" is Norman Knox's term, "On the Classification of Ironies," *Modern Philology* 70 (1972): 53–62, to indicate the area in which irony is noticed.

44. Norman Knox, "Irony," in *Dictionary of the History of Ideas*, ed. P. P. Weiner (New York: Charles Scribner's Sons, 1973), 2:629.

45. For representative works, see F. Schlegel, *Kritische Schriften*, ed. W. Rasch (Munich: C. Hanswer, 1956), *Literary Notebooks, 1779–1801*, ed. H. Eichner (Toronto: Univ. of Toronto Press, 1957); A. W. Schlegel, *Kritische Schriften*, ed. E. Staiger (Zurich: Artemis Verlag, 1962); idem, *A Course of Lectures on Dramatic Art and Literature*, trans. J. Black (Philadelphia: Hogan and Thompson, 1833); K. Solger, *Vorlesungen über Ästhetic*, ed. K. W. L. Heyse (Darmstadt: Wissenschaftliche Buchgesellschaft, 1962). The most complete analysis of German

Romantic irony is Ingrid Strohschneider-Kohrs, *Die Romantische Ironie in Theorie und Gestaltung* (Tübingen: Max Niemeyer Verlag, 1960).

46. Muecke, *Compass,* 191.

47. This vision of life and language can be seen in the plays of Samuel Beckett, Harold Pinter, Jean Genet, and Eugene Ionesco and in the fiction of Jorge Luis Borges and Alain Robbe-Grillet. For a discussion of the modern vision, see Arnold L. Weinstein, *Vision and Response in Modern Fiction* (Ithaca, N.Y.: Cornell Univ. Press, 1974) and Alan Wilde, *Horizons of Assent, Modernism, Postmodernism, and the Ironic Imagination* (Baltimore: Johns Hopkins Univ. Press, 1981).

48. Thomas Mann is the most outstanding example of an author whose fiction was influenced by romantic irony.

49. Cervantes was admired for his ability to sustain irony throughout a narrative and for the way he used authorial intrusion in *Don Quixote,* Shakespeare for the way he created ironic tension by juxtaposing the comic and the tragic and for the posture of both creative involvement and distance that his works present. See Knox, "Irony," 629–31.

50. Bishop Connop Thirlwall, "On the Irony of Sophocles," in *The Philological Museum* (Cambridge: Deightons, 1833), 2:483–537 [reprinted in *Remains Literary and Theological of Connop Thirlwall,* ed. J. J. Stewart Perowne, vol. 3 (London: Daldy, Isbister, & Co., 1878), 1–57]. Citations are from the Perowne edition.

51. Ibid., 1–8.

52. Ibid., 9.

53. Ibid., 11.

54. Ibid., 19.

55. Ibid., 45–50.

56. Ibid., 1.

57. A study of the irony of the Old Testament lends support to this statement. The ancient Hebrews had no explicit word for irony, yet many of their writings reveal a highly developed sense of irony both as literary device and literary vision. See, for example, E. M. Good, *Irony in the Old Testament* (Philadelphia: Westminster Press, 1965), and James G. Williams, "Irony and Lament: Clues to Prophetic Consciousness," *Semeia* 8 (1977): 51–74.

58. Eleanor Hutchens, *Irony in Tom Jones* (University, Ala.: Univ. of Alabama Press, 1965), 37–38.

59. Muecke (*Compass,* 44) notes the limitation of the expression "verbal irony," preferring in its place the expression "being ironical."

60. For a discussion of this point from a linguistic perspective, see Michel Clyne, "Einige Überlegungen zu einer Linguistik der Ironie," *Zeitschrift für deutsche Philologie* 93 (1974): 345. Clyne presents the encoding of the irony and the anticipation of its comprehension as two simultaneous actions on the part of the person creating the irony.

NOTES

61. Booth, *Rhetoric of Irony,* 6.

62. "Finite" is also one of Booth's marks of stable irony (*Rhetoric of Irony,* 6).

63. Ibid., ix.

64. Booth (ibid., xiv) identifies the central question of the rhetorical study as "how authors and readers achieve irony together." This view is not completely foreign to the traditional view of rhetoric, for the classical rhetoricians were also concerned with the relationship created between speaker and audience by irony, but they were interested in only one aspect of this relationship—how best to convince someone of your point.

65. Muecke, *Compass,* 21.

66. For examples of rhetoricians who classified irony under allegory, see Knox, *The Word Irony,* 6, 10–11, 35–37.

67. Vladimir Jankélévitch, *L'Ironie* (Paris: Flammarion, 1964 [1936]).

68. Booth (*Rhetoric of Irony,* 25) illustrates this point with an excellent example: "One can see this clearly in talking with children who have read C. S. Lewis's Narnia books without being aware of the Christian allegory. To talk explicitly of the death and rebirth of the lion as 'like the story of Christ' neither surprises the child nor offends him; a mild additional pleasure is added, but the essential experience remains the same."

69. Muecke, *Compass,* 20.

70. Reuben Brower, *The Fields of Light: An Experiment in Critical Reading* (New York: Oxford Univ. Press, 1951), 50. For an excellent discussion of the relationship between metaphor and irony and how to read them, see Brower's entire third chapter, "Saying One Thing and Meaning Another (Design in Metaphor and Irony)."

71. The terms "tenor" and "vehicle", quite common in metaphor study, come from the work of I. A. Richards, *The Philosophy of Rhetoric* (London: Oxford Univ. Press, 1936).

72. One can find examples of metaphor in which there is some tension between the two levels of meaning, e.g., in Shakespeare's sonnet, "My Mistress' Eyes." (See the discussion of this poem in Booth, *Rhetoric of Irony,* 123–25.) In such cases, however, the tension arises because the metaphors are used ironically, not from the nature of metaphor. As we shall discuss later (pp. 24–25), any literary form may be used ironically.

73. Paul Werth ("The Linguistics of Double-Vision," *Journal of Literary Semantics* 6 (1977): 3–28) provides a typical example of this view. He writes (p. 25), "*irony* discards one structure in favour of the other, in accordance with textual indications and/or cultural assumptions; *metaphor* thoroughly merges the twin structures together in accordance with certain restrictions on the transfer." Booth (*Rhetoric of Irony,* 22–23) also uses this mathematical analogy in discussing metaphor and irony (see also n. 74 below).

74. Muecke, *Compass,* 53. Booth shows some ambivalence on this point. His mathematical analogy for metaphor and irony and his reconstruction meta-

phor, in which the reading of irony is represented as a process of substituting one set of meanings for another (*Rhetoric of Irony,* 34–37), seem to ignore the fact that the two levels of irony must be held together. Yet he can also write (p. 178), "But irony in a curious way feeds both [the conviction that 'there is more here than meets the eye' and the suspicion that there is less] while in a sense pretending to feed only the second."

75. Muecke, *Compass,* 29. (Muecke attributes this remark to Allan Rodway.)

76. Claudette Kemper, "Irony Anew with Occasional Reference to Byron and Browning," *Studies in English Literature* 7 (1967): 705.

77. Cleanth Brooks and Robert Penn Warren, eds., *Understanding Fiction,* 2d. ed. (New York: Appleton-Century-Crofts, Inc., 1959), 685 (Irony), 686 (Paradox).

78. John 1:15 (cf. John 1:30). A similar paradox is found in the famous line from Wordsworth's poem, "My Heart Leaps Up"—"The Child is father of the Man"—a statement that could be used ironically but in its context is not.

79. Muecke, "Analysis de l'ironie," *Poetique* 36 (1978): 480.

80. The obvious exception to this is the extremely overt ironic statement, "Isn't it ironic that . . . ," when no responsibility for detection is given to the reader.

81. Muecke, *Compass,* 66.

82. Muecke, "Irony Markers," *Poetics* 7 (1978): 365.

83. These three divisions are suggested by Muecke ("Irony Markers," 366).

84. Ibid., 367.

85. One can think, for example, of much of the irony of the Old Testament prophets in which the ideal conduct of the people is juxtaposed with their actual conduct.

86. Booth, *Rhetoric of Irony,* 53–54.

87. D. H. Green, "On Recognizing Medieval Irony," in *The Uses of Criticism,* ed. A. P. Foulkes (Bern: Herbert Lang, 1976), 11–55. Green refers to these signals as "non-verbal signals to irony," which is a misnomer along the same lines as Hutchen's distinction between verbal and substantial irony. For Green's full discussion of these and other "non-verbal" signals, see pp. 35–54.

88. Booth (*Rhetoric of Irony,* 1–3) tells an amusing anecdote about one of his graduate students who erroneously interpreted one of Mr. Bennet's sayings as non-ironic and thus grossly misinterpreted a scene. Booth is dumbfounded that someone could miss Mr. Bennet's ironies, since he is so consistently ironic.

89. For a discussion of Henry Tilney's function in *Northanger Abbey,* see Marvin Mudrick, *Jane Austen, Irony as Defense and Discovery* (Princeton: Princeton Univ. Press, 1952), 37–59.

90. Paul Duke, *Irony in the Fourth Gospel,* chap. 4, is helpful in identifying signals to irony in the Fourth Gospel.

91. *Institutio* 8.6.57.

92. Muecke, "Irony Markers," 374.

93. Booth, *Rhetoric of Irony*, 13.

94. Sedgewick, *Of Irony*, 49.

95. Booth, *Rhetoric of Irony*, 27. Does this emphasis on the building of amiable communities oversimplify the issue? The work of Frank Kermode, in particular *The Genesis of Secrecy: On the Interpretation of Narrative* (Cambridge: Harvard Univ. Press, 1979), offers a quite different approach to this question from that offered by Booth. Kermode's focus is on narrative in general, not the specific narrative device of irony, but his argument has relevance for the discussion of irony. In a discussion of parable theory in the Gospel of Mark, Kermode writes, "Mark is a strong witness to the enigmatic and exclusive character of narrative, to its property of banishing interpreters from its secret places" (pp. 33–34). That a narrative possesses "hermeneutical potential" is just another way of saying that a narrative "must be obscure" (p. 45). Kermode sees the creation of outsiders, of *victims*, as an intentional and inevitable part of narrative art. Using the New Testament parable as his example, Kermode concludes that "parable, it seems, may proclaim truth as a herald does, and at the same time conceal truth like an oracle" (p. 47). Is there a similar obscurantist and exclusionary intent in the use of irony? Booth places such emphasis on the intentional community building side of irony that he ignores this potentially darker side of irony—are there readers who are *intentionally* screened out in order to establish a community? This will be an important question for us to keep in mind as we analyze John's use of irony as revelatory language.

96. Booth, *Rhetoric of Irony*, 28–29.

97. For the classic and generative statement regarding performative language, see J. L. Austin, *How to Do Things with Words* (Cambridge: Harvard Univ. Press, 1962). This book is the William James Lectures delivered at Harvard University in 1955.

98. Wayne Booth, "The Pleasures and Pitfalls of Irony: Or, Why Can't You Say What You Mean?" in *Rhetoric, Philosophy, and Literature: An Exploration*, ed. Don M. Burks (West Lafayette, Ind.: Purdue Univ. Press, 1978), 12.

99. Arthur Sidgwick, "On Some Forms of Irony in Literature," *Cornhill Magazine*, 3d. series, 22 (1907): 499.

100. Good, *Irony in the Old Testament*, 27.

101. Jankélévitch, *L'Ironie*, 66. The italics in the first phrase are Jankélévitch's, those in the second phrase mine.

102. Booth, *Rhetoric of Irony*, 29.

CHAPTER 2. REVELATION IN
THE FOURTH GOSPEL

1. There is an important textual variant in this verse. Major textual witnesses (including P66 and P75) read "only begotten God" *(theos)* in place of "only begotten Son" *(huios)*, and *theos* is the reading adopted by the 26th

Nestle edition. For a recent discussion of John 1:18 and its variants, see D. A. Fennema, "John 1:18: 'God the only Son,'" *NTS* 31 (1985): 124–35.

2. Ernst Haenchen, *John 1,* Hermeneia (Philadelphia: Fortress Press, 1984), 121, 125, notes the transitional function of John 1:18 in connecting the prologue with the Gospel.

3. David H. Kelsey, *The Uses of Scripture in Recent Theology* (Philadelphia: Fortress Press, 1975).

4. Ibid., 161–63.

5. For an excellent example of this understanding of Johannine revelation, see Bernhard Weiss, *Biblical Theology of the New Testament,* trans. J. E. Duguid, 3d rev. ed. (Edinburgh: T. & T. Clark, 1883), 2: 352–57.

6. Weiss, *Biblical Theology,* 357.

7. See, e.g., J. M. Boice, *Witness and Revelation in the Fourth Gospel* (Grand Rapids: Zondervan, 1970). Much of Ernst Haenchen's work is also in line with this approach to revelation: "Probleme des johanneischen 'Prologs'" *ZTK* 56 (1959): 305–34; "Der Vater, der mich gesandt hat," *NTS* 9 (1963): 109–216. Haenchen focuses on the nature of God's love and God's grace, which are made known in Jesus' revelation. See Haenchen's commentary on the *Gospel of John,* 2 vols., Hermeneia (Philadelphia: Fortress Press, 1984).

8. Again see Bernhard Weiss as an example of this approach to the content of revelation: *Biblical Theology,* 2: 384–404, and *The Religion of the New Testament,* trans. G. H. Schodde (New York: Funk & Wagnalls, 1905), 20–40.

9. Oscar Cullman, *Salvation in History* (New York: Harper & Row, 1967), 270. The work of Oscar Cullman is the most important and influential modern statement of this approach to revelation. He develops his argument with particular reference to the Fourth Gospel (ibid., 268–91 and "L'Evangile Johannique at L'Histoire du Salut", *NTS* 11 [1965]: 111–22).

10. For a discussion of the place of the history-of-religions school and its successors in New Testament scholarship, see Part V of Werner G. Kümmel, *The New Testament: The History of the Investigation of its Problems,* trans. S. Maclean Gilmour and H. C. Kee (Nashville: Abingdon Press, 1972), 206–324.

11. A major development in the history-of-religions interpretation of the Fourth Gospel was Mark Lidzbarski's translation of major Mandaean texts into German (*Das Johannesbuch der Mandaër,* 1925). Kurt Rudolph continues to pursue Mandaean influence: see esp., *Die Mandaër,* 2 vols., Vol. 1, *Prolegomena: Das Mandaërproblem,* FRLANT, n.s. 56 (Göttingen: Vandenhoeck & Ruprecht, 1961); and *Gnosis: The Nature of Gnosticism,* trans. R. McL. Wilson (New York: Harper & Row, 1983). For discussions of the interplay between the Fourth Gospel and Qumran, see Herbert Braun, "Qumran und das Neue Testament," *ThR* 28 (1962), esp. 192–234; and Raymond E. Brown, "The Qumran Scrolls and the Johannine Gospel and Epistles," in *The Scrolls and the New Testament,* ed. Krister Stendahl (New York: Harper & Row, 1957), 183–207. The work done by James M. Robinson and his colleagues on the Nag Hammadi corpus, *The Nag Hammadi Library,* ed. James M. Robinson (New York:

NOTES

Harper & Row, 1977), has opened up more avenues for comparative approaches to the Fourth Gospel. For a recent important discussion of Gnosticism and the New Testament, see *The New Testament and Gnosis: Essays in Honour of Robert McL. Wilson*, ed. A. H. B. Logan and A. J. M. Wedderburn (Edinburgh: T. & T. Clark, 1983). For an overview of the history-of-religions approach to the Fourth Gospel, see Robinson, "The Johannine Trajectory," in *Trajectories through Early Christianity*, by James M. Robinson and Helmut Koester, (Philadelphia: Fortress Press, 1971), 260–66.

12. Wilhelm Heitmüller and Wilhelm Bousset made important early contributions in this area of research. See Heitmüller, "Das Johannes-evangelium" in *Die Schriften des Neuen Testaments*, ed. Johannes Weiss (Göttingen: Vandenhoeck & Ruprecht, 1908), 2: 685–861: and Bousset, "Das Johannes-evangelium," in *R.G.G.* [1], 3: 608–36,; idem, *Kyrios Christos, Geschichte des Christus-glaubens von den Anfangen des Christentums bei Irenaeus* (Göttingen: Vandenhoeck & Ruprecht, 1913), chap. 5; ET: *Kyrios Christos*, trans. J. E. Steely (Nashville: Abingdon Press, 1970).

13. Rudolf Bultmann and Walter Bauer are the two scholars most responsible for the initial contributions of this particular approach to the Fourth Gospel. Bauer's work is found in the second edition of his commentary on John, *Das Johannes-Evangelium*, HNT (Tübingen: J. C. B. Mohr, 1925). Bultmann's initial work in this area is found in two early articles, "Der religions-geschichtliche Hintergrund des Prologs zum Johannesevangelium," in *Eucharisterion*, Festschrift for Hermann Gunkel, ed. Hans Schmidt, FRLANT, n.f. 19 (Göttingen: Vandenhoeck & Ruprecht, 1923), 2: 1–26; idem, "Die Bedeutung der neuerschlossen mandaischen und manischaischen Quellen für das Verstandnis des Johannes-evangeliums," *ZNW* 24 (1925): 100–146.

14. Bultmann, "Die Bedeutung," 105–39.

15. Kelsey (*Uses of Scripture*, 74–85) provides a helpful discussion of the existentialist understanding of revelation.

16. For a fuller discussion of the grounds on which Bultmann reaches this conclusion, see his "Das Johannesevangelium in der neuesten Forschung," *Der Christliche Welt* 41 (1927): 502–11, and "Die Bedeutung."

17. Rudolf Bultmann, *The Gospel of John* (Philadelphia: Westminster Press, 1971), 63–66.

18. Rudolf Bultmann, *Theology of the New Testament* (New York: Charles Scribner's Sons, 1955), 2: 46.

19. Ibid., 41; Bultmann, *John*, 83, 605.

20. Bultmann, *Theology*, 66.

21. Ibid., 58. Bultmann's attitude toward history and salvation had a significant impact on his understanding of the relationship between the Old and New Testaments. See "The Significance of the Old Testament for Christian Faith," in *The Old Testament and Christian Faith*, ed. Bernhard W. Anderson (New York: Harper & Row, 1963), 8–35.

22. Bultmann's concepts of myth and demythologizing are intimately con-

nected to his theology of revelation. Bultmann viewed myth as any language which objectified God, God's words, or God's actions, and he saw the Fourth Evangelist's treatment of the gnostic redeemer myth—stripping it down to the bare existential encounter—as evidence that a New Testament writer also viewed myth as objective language about God. H. P. Owen ("Revelation," in *The Theology of Rudolf Bultmann*, ed. C. W. Kegley [New York: Harper & Row, 1966], 45) draws attention to the relationship between myth and revelation for Bultmann, and Bultmann ("Reply to H. P. Owen, 'Revelation' " in the same volume) expresses his gratitude for a correct interpretation of this relationship: "I am especially grateful that, in view of misunderstandings, Owen shows how my concept of myth and demythologizing is determined by my understanding of revelation . . . " (p. 261).

23. Bultmann, *John*, 308.

24. Ernst Käsemann, *The Testament of Jesus According to John 17* (Philadelphia: Fortress Press, 1968). Only the first two sections, "The Glory of Christ" and "The Community under the Word" directly pertain to the question of revelation. The work of Josef Blank, *Krisis. Untersuchungen zur johanneischen Christologie und Eschatologie* (Freiburg: Lambertus-Verlag, 1964), could also be classified under the dogmatic approach to revelation. Blank's work has many points of contact with Käsemann. For a fuller discussion of Blank, see Gail R. O'Day, *Irony and the Johannine Theology of Revelation. An Investigation of John 4*, (Ph.D. diss., Emory University, 1983), 29–33.

25. Käsemann, *Testament*, 23.

26. Ibid., 24.

27. Ibid., 25.

28. Ibid.

29. Käsemann states this locus quite explicitly in *The Testament of Jesus* (p. 26): "An undogmatic faith is, at the very least, a decision against the Fourth Gospel."

30. The influence of the *Dass/Was* distinction can be seen clearly, as already noted, in the shape the dogmatic approach to revelation in the Fourth Gospel takes. The *Dass/Was* distinction also establishes the categories for the work of Boice and Haenchen. For a discussion of the pervasive influence of this distinction, see O'Day, *Irony and Theology*, (pp. 11–48), and "Narrative Mode and Theological Claim: A Study in the Fourth Gospel," *JBL* (forthcoming).

31. Bultmann, *John*, 201.

32. L. Cerfaux ("Le thème littéraire parabolique dans l'Evangile de Saint Jean," *CN* 11 Festschrift for Anton Fridrichsen [Lund: G. W. K. Gleerup, 1947], 15–25) studied Johannine revelatory language as parabolic language.

33. H. Leroy (*Rätsel und Missverständnis. Ein Beitrag zum Formgeschichte des Johannesevangeliums* [Bonn: Peter Hanstein, 1968]) identifies eleven instances of misunderstanding in John and classifies them as riddles.

34. R. Alan Culpepper, *Anatomy of the Fourth Gospel.*

35. For a recent discussion on the importance of explicit methodological and hermeneutical awareness in literary analysis of biblical texts, see John Barton, *Reading the Old Testament: Method in Biblical Study* (Philadelphia: Westminster Press, 1984). Barton raises valuable questions about the ways in which we interpret texts.

36. Wayne Meeks, "The Man from Heaven in Johannine Sectarianism," *JBL* 91 (1972): 44–72.

37. It is interesting to compare Meeks' understanding of what functions as warrants for Jesus' revelation with Käsemann's understanding of the Father/Son language of the Fourth Gospel as the warrants for Jesus' revelation.

38. Meeks, "Man from Heaven," 57.

39. Ibid., 68–69.

40. Ibid., 69. Meeks' main concern, however, is not with the precise nature of Johannine revelatory language but with what the function of Johannine revelatory language that he has noted says about the nature of the Johannine community.

41. For a discussion of the world-creating power of story, see Amos N. Wilder, "Story and Story-World," *Int* 37 (1983): 353–64.

CHAPTER 3. REVELATION IN CONTEXT
(JOHN 4:4–42)

1. Bultmann, for example, posited that Jesus' dialogue with the woman was the original core of the chapter, and that it had been drawn from the *semeia* source. He located the source material in vv. 5–7, 9ab, 16–19, 28–30, 40. Bultmann considered Jesus' dialogue with the disciples to be a secondary addition by the evangelist, to whom he attributed the rest of the material in the chapter, with the exception of vv. 9c and 22b which he viewed as editorial glosses (*John*, pp. 178, 180). More recently, see Robert Fortna, *The Gospel of Signs. A Reconstruction of the Narrative Source Underlying the Fourth Gospel* (Cambridge: Cambridge Univ. Press, 1970), 193–94. He has found material in John 4 which he feels has been drawn from the *semeia* gospel. The original source story that Fortna postulates is almost identical with that suggested by Bultmann: vv. 4–7, 9ab, 16–19, 25, 26, 29–30, 40,(42).

2. Fortna, *Gospel of Signs*, 189.

3. Ibid., 190.

4. An interpretation at the opposite end of the scale from ours is that of Luise Schottroff, "Johannes 4.5–15 und die Konsequenzen des johanneischen Dualismus," *ZNW* 60 (1969): 199–214. Schottroff's dualistic interpretation of this passage is dependent on a particular source-critical view of the text. John 4:5–7, 9 constitute the original pre-Johannine story, which deals with the issue of Samaritan/Jewish hatred, an *"innerweltlichen"* concern. Verses 10–15, by contrast, are Johannine and deal with eternal life, something which has

a negative relation to earthly life and its concerns. The breach between these two views, made clear because they stem from different hands, is irresolvable. Schottroff can only maintain this starkly dualistic interpretation of John 4:5–15 because of the source-critical theories to which she adheres.

5. In an early analysis of John 4:1–42, Lothar Schmid ("Die Komposition der Samaria-Szene John 4:1–42," *ZNW* 28 [1929]: 148–58) noted the progression of titles in this scene. See Rudolf Schnackenburg, *The Gospel According to John,* trans. K. Smyth (New York: Crossroad, 1982 [1968]), 1: 410; he notes a similar pattern of progressive titles.

6. Gerhard Friedrich, *Wer ist Jesus? Die Verkündigung des vierten Evangelisten, dargestellt an Johannes 4.4–42* (Stuttgart: Calver Verlag, 1967). In this insightful analysis of John 4, Friedrich touches upon the interrelationship of form and content in Jesus' revelation in this chapter.

7. Schnackenburg *(John)* begins his analysis with 4:1 and sees 4:1–5 as the entire introduction. Birger Olsson in *Structure and Meaning in the Fourth Gospel. A Text-Linguistic Analysis of John 2:1–11 and 4:1–42,* ConBNT 6 (Lund: GWK Gleerup, 1974) begins with 4:1–4 as the introduction. Raymond E. Brown, in *The Gospel According to John I–XII,* Anchor Bible 29 (Garden City, N.Y.: Doubleday & Co., 1966) takes 4:4 as the beginning of the Samaria narrative. Edwyn Clement Hoskyns, *The Fourth Gospel,* ed. F. N. Davey, 2d ed. (London: Faber & Faber, 1947), begins with v. 5.

8. Brown *(John,* 164–65) also identifies this section as transitional.

9. The movement in the early and middle stages of the narrative of all the characters *except* Jesus helps to underscore the centrality of the figure of Jesus. One could compare the detailed narration of movement in this scene with John's narration of the trial before Pilate. In that scene Jesus becomes the focal point as John deliberately narrates his movements inside and outside of the praetorium. Here the other characters' movements are deliberately narrated, thus isolating Jesus as the one constant and hence the focal point.

10. Much has been written about the two-stage technique in John. It is used here not in the sense of Martyn *(History and Theology)* but in that of C. H. Dodd, *The Interpretation of the Fourth Gospel* (Cambridge: Cambridge Univ. Press, 1953), 315. Olsson *(Structure and Meaning,* 138ff.) has done extensive work on the two-scene composition of this narrative.

11. See P. J. Cahill, "Narrative Art in John IV," *Religious Studies Bulletin* 2 (1982): 43. He accurately notes that the actual movement of Jesus from the well to the Samaritan town is not narrated. Cahill reads too much into this narrative detail, however, noting that it gives an "eery credence" to the Samaritan confession of 4:42 and that it is a "clarification of the assertion that 'God is spirit.' "

12. Olsson, *Structure and Meaning,* 139.

13. The plausibility of this reading is supported by Josephus, *Antiquities*

20.115; *Jewish War* 2.32; *Life* 269, who suggests that the way through Samaria was the shortest route.

14. Brown (*John,* 169) and Olsson (*Structure and Meaning,* 145) answer this question in the affirmative, whereas C. K. Barrett (*The Gospel According to John,* 2d ed. [Philadelphia: Westminster Press, 1978], 230) interprets this expression solely in terms of the geographical evidence.

15. Genesis 33:19 and 48:22 mention that Jacob bought land at Shechem and gave it to Joseph, but Genesis nowhere makes mention of the well. Jacob is associated with Laban's well at Haran, however, and rabbinic traditions developed which depict Jacob as performing a miracle at the well and which may lie behind the woman's question in 4:12. Cf. Jose Ramon Diaz, "Palestinian Targum and New Testament," *NovT* 6 (1963): 76–77 and Jerome H. Neyrey, S.J., "Jacob Traditions and the Interpretation of John 4:10–26," *CBQ* 42 (1979): 421–25.

16. Attempts have been made to give symbolic significance to this phrase, but they do not seem justified by the text. For a summary of many of these attempts, see Olsson, *Structure and Meaning,* 150–51. Culpepper suggests that the reference "the sixth hour" should be counted according to the Roman, not the Jewish system of time (*Anatomy of The Fourth Gospel,* 219). In that case, Jesus arrives at evening and is tired from a long day's journey.

17. See Hans-Martin Schenke, "Jakobsbrunnen-Josephsgrab-Sychar," *ZDPV* 84 (1968): 166ff. He argues that this site was a shrine.

18. Olsson, *Structure and Meaning,* 141.

19. Ibid., 173. Olsson divides the dialogue into its component speeches: v. 7, v. 9, v. 10, v. 11, v. 13, v. 15, v. 16, v. 17, v. 19, v. 21, v. 25, v. 26.

20. C. H. Dodd, "The Dialogue Form in the Gospels," *BJRL* 37 (1954): 62; Friedrich, *Wer ist Jesus?,* 26.

21. The role of v. 8 in uniting the plot lines of the Samaritan woman and the disciples has already been discussed (see p. 53). We can see here that it also makes a contribution to the Samaritan story line proper.

22. Olsson (*Structure and Meaning,* 177) notes that the participial construction of this verse in the Greek gives it a certain symmetry.

23. Bultmann, *John,* 178.

24. See, e.g., 11:49–52. After Caiaphas unconsciously prophesies about the expediency of Jesus' death for the salvation of the people, John repeats his words almost verbatim.

25. The discussion has focused on whether or not sugchraomai refers to general social interaction or specific ritual impurity. For two contrasting views, see David Daube, "Jesus and the Samaritan Woman: The Meaning of συγχράομαι," *JBL* 69 (1950): 137–47; and D. R. Hall, "The Meaning of συγχράομαι in John 4:9," *ExpTim* 83 (1971–72): 56–57.

26. Olsson, *Structure and Meaning,* 179.

27. Schnackenburg (*John,* 1: 426) points to the loose chiastic structure of the verse in which the gift of God is balanced by living water.

28. Friedrich, *Wer ist Jesus?,* 31.

29. Schweizer, *Ego Eimi,* 161; François Vouga, *Le cadre historique et l'intention theologique de Jean* (Paris: Editions Beauchesne, 1977), 28.

30. Meeks, *The Prophet-King. Moses Tradition and the Johannine Christology* (Leiden: E. J. Brill, 1967), 38.

31. Paul S. Minear, " 'We Don't Know Where . . . ' John 20:2" *Int* 30 (1976): 131–32; Duke, *Irony in the Fourth Gospel,* 64–72.

32. See, e.g., Schmid, "Die Komposition der Samaria-Szene," 250; Brown, *John,* 170; Barrett, *John,* 234; Olsson, *Structure and Meaning,* 180; Lindars, *John,* 182. Barnabas Lindars, *The Gospel of John,* New Century Bible (Grand Rapids: Mich.: Wm. B. Eerdmans, 1981 [1972]), 182.

33. Olsson, *Structure and Meaning,* 180; Duke, *Irony in the Fourth Gospel,* 70.

34. Duke, *Irony in the Fourth Gospel,* 72–73.

35. Neyrey ("Jacob Traditions," 424–25) suggests that what is at issue in this verse is Jesus' supplanting of Jacob the supplanter. While this would add to the irony of 4:12, it seems unlikely. For a similar response to Neyrey's suggestion, see Duke, *Irony in the Fourth Gospel,* 70, n. 19.

36. Lindars, *John,* 182–83.

37. Ibid.

38. It is therefore inaccurate to call 4:12 an unanswered question (so Culpepper, *Anatomy of the Fourth Gospel,* 176). There are instances in John where the evangelist offers no response to questions and lets silence speak, but in vv. 13–14 he does offer an indirect answer to the question in v. 12.

39. Schnackenburg, *John,* 1: 430–32.

40. In the history of interpretation of this verse, *hydōr zōn* has been understood as referring either to the spirit or the revelation brought by Jesus. The case for reading *hydōr zōn* as spirit is supported by John 7:37–39, where John explicitly interprets Jesus' words about living water as referring to the spirit. In 7:37, however, one drinks from Jesus, while in 4:14 one drinks from the water offered by Jesus. The case for reading *hydōr zōn* as Jesus' revelation is based primarily on the parallel functions of the bread of life in John 6 and the water of life here, both understood as Jesus' gift to humanity, his revelation. It has become increasingly clear in contemporary scholarship, however, that these two interpretations are not mutually exclusive. For John, the spirit and the revelation of Jesus are intimately connected. See Francis J. McCool, "Living Water in John," in *The Bible in Current Catholic Thought,* ed. J. C. McKenzie (New York: Herder & Herder, 1962), 226–33, and Schnackenburg, *John,* 1:431–32. See also the discussion of 4:20–24 below.

41. So, Brown, *John,* 177.

42. See my chap. 1, p. 17 n. 36 above.

43. In many ways, the woman's coherent dialogue resembles the "coherent story" (Fortna) of the source critics.

44. It is incorrect to assume that the evangelist just neglected to narrate the woman's offer of water to Jesus. So J. H. Bernard, *The Gospel According to John,* ICC (Edinburgh: T. & T. Clark, 1929), 137.

45. Bernard (*John,* 1:143) explains the request by saying that only a fragment of the conversation has been preserved and "much that was said is, no doubt, omitted in the narration of John." Lindars (*John,* 185) suggests that Jesus hopes to make the woman realize that he is not speaking about physical water by telling her that what he has said applies to her husband as well as to her. F. Roustang ("Les moments de l'acte de foi et ses conditions de possibilite. Essai d'interpretation du dialogue avec la Samaritaine," *RSR* 46 [1958]: 349) explains that this exchange takes place in order to bring the woman to an awareness of her status as a sinner, a prerequisite to receiving Jesus' revelation. Similarly, on the basis of 2 Kings 17:24–31, an allegorical explanation of this shift of topic is proposed. The five husbands stand for the gods of the five nations mentioned in 2 Kings, and the exchange is thus a reflection on the illegitimate forms of Samaritan worship. This is a perennially popular view, defended most recently by Olsson (*Structure and Meaning,* 186) and Cahill ("Narrative Art," 44).

46. Roustang ("Les moments de l'acte de foi," 362) notes the opposition between the uses of *enthade* in vv. 15 and 16.

47. Note, as in vv. 7–15, the repetition of one speech in another. Here the repeated saying is "have/do not have a husband."

48. F. Godet, *Commentaire sur L'Evangile de Saint Jean* (Paris: Libraire Francaise et Étrangère, 1864), 486; and Julius Graf, "Jesus and die Samariterin," *BK* 6 (1951): 107. Both note that vv. 17 and 18 are ironic but do not clarify why the statements are ironic.

49. Duke (*Irony in the Fourth Gospel,* 101–3) has recently used v. 18 to support his interpretation of this meeting between Jesus and the Samaritan woman as an intentionally ironic adaptation of the Old Testament well courtship narratives (Gen. 24:10–61; 29:1–20; Exod. 2:15b–21). Until v. 18, the first-century reader would have recognized the story that he or she was reading as another example of this conventional scene. (Duke draws on Robert Alter, *The Art of Biblical Narrative* [New York: Basic Books, 1981], 51–60, for his description of the conventions involved. Cahill, ["Narrative Art," 45–47] also draws on Alter in describing this scene as a biblical type scene. Cahill, in contrast to Duke, does not feel that the conventions are used ironically.) At v. 18, according to Duke, the irony of the situation is made manifest, however, because it becomes clear that Jesus is not conversing with a virgin at the well (as was typical in the Old Testament stories), but with a "five-time loser." That John is alluding to these well scenes, particularly to the one involving Jacob, is quite likely in the face of all the other patriarchal imagery

on which he draws to establish the Jacob/Jesus contrast. That the narrative was specifically modeled on those stories, however, is unlikely, since the two central elements of the Old Testament stories—the drawing of water and the betrothal—are missing in John 4:4–42. See also Calum C. Carmichael, "Marriage and the Samaritan Woman," *NTS* 26 (1980): 322–46. He argues on theological rather than literary grounds that the Samaria narrative deliberately presents Jesus and the Samaritan woman as husband and wife.

50. Meeks (*The Prophet-King,* 34) notes that Jesus is called "a prophet" twice, 4:19 and 9:17, in each case by someone who in some sense is a paradigm of incipient faith.

51. Duke (*Irony in the Fourth Gospel,* 103) argues that when the woman's true status is revealed, she tries "desperately . . . to put distance between herself and Jesus." Edwyn Clement Hoskyns (*The Fourth Gospel,* ed. F. N. Davey, 2d ed. [London: Faber & Faber 1947], 237, 243) suggests that the woman is seeking information regarding the correct sacred place at which she should pray for forgiveness of her sins, which were exposed by Jesus. An allegorical explanation of this worship theme is also offered: in light of the allegorical interpretation of vv. 16–19, these verses are a continuation, not a change in topic (see, e.g., Cahill, "Narrative Art," 46–47).

52. Brown (*John,* 175) describes the woman as "mincing and coy, with a certain light grace." (See also p. 176, where Brown asks if "a Samaritan woman would have been expected to understand even the most basic ideas of the discourse.") Duke (*Irony in the Fourth Gospel,* 102–3) refers to the woman as a "five-time loser" and a "tramp," while I. Howard Marshall ("The Problem of New Testament Exegesis," *Journal of the Evangelical Theology Society* 17 (1974): 68) describes the woman in the following way: "What visual image does that word [woman/*gunē*] convey to you? To me it is a word which suggests somebody approaching middle-age or even old-age, and it has a faintly derogatory air . . . 'woman' tends to put her on the shelf, but the story implies that she was possibly youthful and attractive." These judgments are not made on the basis of the text itself and certainly provide an obstacle in conceiving of the Samaritan woman as capable of initiating genuine theological discourse.

53. Bultmann, *John,* 189; Schnackenburg, *John,* 1: 434; Olsson, *Structure and Meaning,* 188.

54. Bultmann, *John,* 189.

55. See Duke, *Irony in the Fourth Gospel,* 70.

56. Against Bultmann, *John,* 189, n. 6, Friedrich, *Wer ist Jesus?,* 43; and others, who interpret this distinction in terms of Christians and non-Christians.

57. Bultmann, *John,* 189, n. 6.

58. For example, Friedrich, *Wer ist Jesus?,* 43.

59. Meeks, *The Prophet-King,* 41 n. 2. The geography of the Gospel lends

NOTES

support to this reading of v. 22b. Jesus travels back and forth between Judea and Galilee as he encounters rejection and acceptance. An explicit statement of this tension between the place of origin and the place of acceptance is found in 4:44: "For Jesus himself testified that a prophet has no honor in his own country."

60. Duke, *Irony in the Fourth Gospel,* 64–90, and Culpepper, *Anatomy of the Fourth Gospel,* 169–70.

61. It is unclear whether the official is a pagan or not. However, if one follows Meeks ("Galilee and Judea in the Fourth Gospel," *JBL* 85 [1966]: 159–69) and sees the Galileans (as distinct from the Jews) as those who accept Jesus, the question becomes irrelevant in terms of the official's response to Jesus.

62. Brown (*John,* 181) links this passage with Jesus' replacement of the Jewish temple with his body in 2:13–22.

63. Schnackenburg, *John,* 1: 439.

64. Cf. the Samaritan woman's response with Jesus' conversation with Martha in 11:23–26.

65. That the Jewish term "Messiah" is used by a Samaritan should not be pressed too closely (see Meeks, *The Prophet-King,* 318). The verb *anangelei* does have points of contact with the Samaritan expectation of the *Ta'heb,* that is, "the one who returns."

66. Bultmann, *John,* 192.

67. Siegfried Schulz, *Das Evangelium nach Johannes,* NTD 4 (Göttingen: Vandenhoeck & Ruprecht, 1972), 76.

68. For a discussion of the different types of *egō eimi* sayings in the Fourth Gospel, see Bultmann, *John,* 225 n. 3, and Philip B. Harner, *The "I am" of the Fourth Gospel: A Study in Johannine Usage and Thought* (Philadelphia: Fortress Press, 1970). Barrett, *John,* 238, and Lindars, *John,* 148, maintain that one needs to supply a predicate for the *egō eimi* of 4:26, but such an interpretation diminishes the force of the revelation.

69. George MacRae, "The Fourth Gospel and *Religionsgeschichte,"* CBQ 32 (1970): 23. See also the similar comments of Francis J. Moloney, "From Cana to Cana (John 2:1—4:54) and the Fourth Evangelist's Concept of Correct (and Incorrect) Faith," *Salesianum* 40 (1978): 838. We shall return to this point in our discussion of 4:42.

70. Schnackenburg, *John,* 1: 443.

71. In Mark, the disciples can also be viewed as insiders who ironically become outsiders. For a discussion of this, see Werner Kelber, *Mark's Story of Jesus* (Philadelphia: Fortress Press, 1979), 30–42. By contrast, Duke (*Irony in the Fourth Gospel,* 60) writes that the disciples in John do not become outsiders.

72. The disciples' question in v. 27 is an example of a frequent pattern in the Fourth Gospel: a statement made or question asked *by* Jesus is later directed *to* him. For example, in 1:38 Jesus asks two of John's disciples, "What

do you seek?" In 4:27 this question is asked of him. In 18:4, Jesus again asks, "Who do you seek?" this time of those who come to arrest him. (Cf. 20:25 where the resurrected Jesus asks Mary, "Who do you seek?") Similarly, in 1:39 the invitation "Come and see" is offered by Jesus; in 11:34 this invitation is offered to him (cf. 1:46 and 4:49 where the same invitation is offered about him).

73. Barrett, *John,* 239.

74. Brown, *John,* 273.

75. See Lindars, *John,* 193.

76. Ibid., 179. Hendrikus Boers, "Discourse Structure and Macro-Structure in the Interpretation of Texts: John 4:1–42 as an Example," *Society of Biblical Literature Seminar Papers—1980* (Chico, Calif.: Scholars Press, 1980) 175.

77. See above, 133 n. 72.

78. Schulz, *Das Evangelium nach Johannes,* 77.

79. See Boers, "Discourse Structure and Macro-Structure," 176.

80. It is difficult to see how Olsson (*Structure and Meaning,* 209) can maintain that the woman's response is unequivocal in its affirmation and pronouncement of Jesus.

81. Schnackenburg, *John,* 1: 444.

82. Olsson, *Structure and Meaning,* 148.

83. Fortna (*The Gospel of Signs,* 192) sees this imperfect form, and the delay of the townspeople's arrival which it implies, as evidence of John's disruption of the source material.

84. It is interesting to note that the Samaritan woman is bringing the townspeople back to the well, a place to which she had earlier said she did not want to return (v. 15).

85. The other two private conversations are 1:37–51 and 6:66–71. See Dodd, *Interpretation,* 390.

86. Olsson, *Structure and Meaning,* 221.

87. See discussion of v. 12 above. See Duke, *Irony in the Fourth Gospel,* 97. He surprisingly says that when the disciples do "fall prey to irony," John's grammatical indicators (e.g., the confident use of *mē* in questions) are absent.

88. Olsson, *Structure and Meaning,* 223. He attributes the irony of this verse to the initiated reader's knowledge that Jesus is talking about nonordinary food. He goes on to say that the reader can supply the correct answer to the disciples' question in v. 33. This final statement misreads the situation, because as v. 34 shows, only Jesus can supply the correct answer to their question. The reader, however, can *ask* the question in the right sense.

89. Leroy, *Rätsel und Missverstandnis,* 151–52.

90. *Brōma* occurs only here in the Fourth Gospel.

91. Olsson (*Structure and Meaning,* 251 and passim) stresses the *ergon* aspect of John 4:1–42 throughout his analysis of the text.

92. M. de Jonge, "Jesus as Prophet and King in the Fourth Gospel," in *Jesus:*

Stranger from Heaven and Son of God (Missoula, Mont.: Scholars Press, 1977), 66. Culpepper (*Anatomy of the Fourth Gospel,* 179) says that the Samaritan woman becomes a victim of irony as a result of this exchange between Jesus and his disciples, but the revelation given by Jesus here is not given at the expense of anyone. To see the woman as a victim here is to undervalue the narrative impact of the *egō eimi* in 4:26. See also Dodd, *Interpretation,* 315.

93. Olsson, *Structure and Meaning,* 220.

94. Donatien Mollat, "Le Puits de Jacob (Jean 4, 1–42)," *BVC* 6 (1954): 89. As mentioned before (p. 79), Jesus' response in v. 34 also incorporates aspects of the earlier conversation with the Samaritan woman.

95. See C. H. Dodd, *Historical Tradition in the Fourth Gospel* (Cambridge: Cambridge Univ. Press, 1963), 391. He sees no connection.

96. Hoskyns, *John,* 246. The image of harvest also follows naturally from the image of food (Brown, *John,* 181).

97. This proverb has not been found outside of this text, but it is in keeping with agricultural practice in Palestine.

98. Wilhelm Thüsing, *Die Erhöhung und Verherrlichung Jesu im Johannes-evangelium,* 3d ed. (Münster Westfallen: Aschendorff, 1979), 151.

99. Olsson, *Structure and Meaning,* 226.

100. See above, p. 78.

101. So Lindars, *John,* 195.

102. This presupposes that the *ēdē* is read with v. 36, a reading which makes the most sense and is supported by the textual evidence. Dodd (*Historical Tradition,* 392) draws attention to the temporal differences among the harvest sayings, although he overemphasizes the distinction.

103. Olsson, *Structure and Meaning,* 228.

104. Thüsing, *Die Erhöhung und Verherrlichung Jesu,* 54; Olsson, *Structure and Meaning,* 228; Schnackenburg, *John,* 1:447.

105. Schnackenburg, *John,* 1: 452.

106. The transitional status of v. 37 is readily grasped if the definite article *ho* before both sower and harvester is understood as generic.

107. Dodd, *Historical Tradition,* 392.

108. Bultmann, *John,* 199.

109. The specific referent of the "others" has been a vexed question in the study of v. 38. Raymond Brown ("Roles of Women in the Fourth Gospel," *TS* 36 (1975): 692), for example, suggests that the "others" could imply the Samaritan woman who had prepared her townspeople to meet Jesus. Oscar Cullman ("Samaria and the Origins of the Christian Church. Who are the ἄλλοι of John 4:38?," in *The Early Church,* ed. A. J. B. Higgins [London: SCM Press, 1956], 285–92) argues that the "others" refer to those people in the mission of the early church who laid the missionary groundwork in Samaria. Yet neither of those suggestions seems to capture the extended function of the term in the narrative. It seems best to accept the indefiniteness of the very

expression "others" as part of its intended meaning. Like the proverb of v. 37, this saying has a wide range of applications.

110. See Urban C. von Wahlde, "A Redactional Technique in the Fourth Gospel," *CBQ* 38 (1976): 520–33. He cites this verse as an example of a literary device that he calls a "repetitive resumptive." This literary device "marks off material an editor has inserted and serves to indicate the parenthetical nature of the material" (520). Von Wahlde focuses in particular on texts in John which contain the connectives *hote oun* or *hōs oun.* The presence of the phrase *hōs oun* in 4:40, together with the repetition of the sequence of 4:30, lead von Wahlde to view vv. 40–42 as an editorial insertion to the "basic story" (520–32).

111. Boers, "Discourse Structure and Macro-Structure," 176; Meeks, "Galilee and Judea in the Fourth Gospel," 167.

112. The intensive use of the pronoun *autoi* underlines this, because it emphasizes that *they themselves* have heard.

113. Bultmann, *John,* 201.

114. Barrett, *John,* 243.

115. Schnackenburg, *John,* 1: 457.

116. Ibid.

117. Dodd ("The Dialogue Form," 63) makes a similar comment about all the actors and interlocutors in John.

118. For an important discussion of the role of distance and overhearing in the communication and appropriation of the New Testament, see Fred B. Craddock, *Overhearing the Gospel* (Nashville: Abingdon Press, 1978).

119. Meeks, "The Man from Heaven." 69. See my chap. 2, pp. 46–47.

120. Boers, "Discourse Structure and Macro-Structure," 175.

CHAPTER 4. THE LOCUS
OF REVELATION

1. The question of the relationship between the end of John 20 and John 21 is a complex one. John 20:30–31 clearly has the tone of a conclusion, yet it is followed by another chapter. The scholarly consensus is that chap. 21 should be understood as an appendix to the Gospel proper. For a review of this question, see Brown, *John,* 1057–61, 1077–82. For a recent challenge to this consensus view, see Minear, "The Original Functions of John 21," *JBL* 102 (1983): 85–98.

2. The debate about the intended audience of the purpose clause of John 20:31 is triggered by an important textual variant in the verse. The textual witnesses are divided as to whether one should read *pisteusēte,* an aortist subjunctive, or *pisteuēte,* a present subjunctive. The aorist subjunctive could imply "come to faith" and would support the view of an audience who does not yet believe, whereas the present subjunctive would mean "keep believing" and would therefore suggest an audience of believers. See Brown, *John,*

1056, Schnackenburg, *John,* 3: 337–40. Cf. Bultmann (*John,* 698) who considers such discussion "irrelevant."

3. Bultmann, *John,* 697.

4. MacRae, "Theology and Irony," 88.

5. This understanding of the relationship between deeds and the locus of revelation corresponds well with the Johannine treatment of signs. It is not the signs as miraculous deeds which are the source of faith. The signs must be correctly interpreted, so that the manifestation of glory (2:11) can be rightly perceived.

6. These loci of revelation and what the Fourth Gospel looks like when viewed from these differing perspectives were discussed at length in chap. 2. It is helpful to keep these different rubrics in mind as telling points of contrast with the thesis of this book about the locus of revelation.

7. It is interesting to note that Bultmann himself points toward the "how" of Jesus as revealer. In his insistence on the central paradox of the Gospel, that the *doxa* can only be seen through the *sarx,* Bultmann implies that how one encounters and responds to Jesus is governed by the "how" in which Jesus is made known. Bultmann, however, does not modify his insistence on the bare *Dass* of revelation with this observation. Yet as we noted (p. 6), Bultmann's portrait of the Logos is actually more ironical than paradoxical and indicates that it is only by interpreting the ironic double image of *sarx/doxa* that one is able to experience Jesus as revealer. The mode of revelation is an essential part of the revelation experience.

8. Scholars who stress the role of imagination in biblical texts are Amos N. Wilder, William A. Beardslee, Paul Ricoeur, David Tracy, Walter Brueggemann, and Sallie McFague.

9. Wolfgang Iser, *The Act of Reading. A Theory of Aesthetic Response* (Baltimore: Johns Hopkins Univ. Press, 1978), 142.

10. While one might want to argue with the more absolute claims of the phenomenology of reading (e.g., there is no meaning until the reader creates it), its emphasis on reader response is very important for the study of irony. Iser represents a moderate position, noting that the meaning that the reader creates is very carefully structured into the text (ibid., 38, 39).

11. What the reader *does not* know can also draw the reader into the text. In John 4:16–19 it is the reader's ignorance of the Samaritan woman's marital status that brings the reader to a direct experience of Jesus' omniscience (see pp. 66–67).

12. The similarities between John 4 and 6 have given rise to a displacement theory about the original order of this section of the Fourth Gospel. Bultmann argued that the original order of John 4—7 was 4, 6, 5, 7. This theory of rearrangement has been more widely followed than any other displacement hypothesis suggested for the Fourth Gospel. See, for example, Schnackenburg (*John,* 2: 1–9) who accepts this displacement theory.

13. Compare also the transformation of "give" in John 4 (see p. 64).

14. Schnackenburg, *John,* 2: 36.

15. Cf. John 4:34.

16. That this passage in John is an example of Jewish midrashic technique is the central thesis of Peder Borgen, *Bread from Heaven* (Leiden: E. J. Brill, 1965).

17. Borgen, *Bread from Heaven,* 61–69, discusses the "exegetical pattern of contrast" in these verses.

18. For a discussion of this verse and its significance for the Johannine ascent/descent motif, see Meeks, "Man from Heaven."

19. See, e.g., Barrett, *John,* 291; Brown, *John,* 267; Schnackenburg, *John,* 2: 43; Borgen, *Bread from Heaven,* 69.

20. Dodd (*Interpretation,* 416) is an exception to this consensus view. He limits the referent of *en paroimiais* to 16:19–22.

21. E.g., Brown, *John,* 735; Schnackenburg, *John,* 3: 192; Cerfaux, "Le thème littéraire", 26.

22. Luis Rubio Moran, "Revelacion en enigmas y revelacion en claridad," *Salmanticensis* 19 (1972): 118. This is in contrast to the two other occurrences of *paroimia* in addition to 16:25, 10:6, and 16:29, where the noun is used in the singular and refers to individual teaching units.

23. Ibid.

24. To this view of "in figures", cf. Mark 4:11, 34.

25. E.g., Brown, *John,* 736; Schnackenburg, *John,* 3: 162; Cerfaux, "Le thème littéraire", 26, and Moran, "Revelacion," 124. Cf. William Wrede (*Das Messiasgeheimnis in den Evangelien* [ET: *The Messianic Secret,* Cambridge: James Clarke, 1971 (1901), 190]) who interprets this verse in terms of his understanding of the Messianic secret.

26. Booth (*Rhetoric of Irony,* 55) makes the following comment about direct clues in ironic texts: "It is foolish to ignore them when they are offered, but it is dangerous to take them at face value. They may or may not be reliable clues to what the work achieves. The author, for all we know in advance, may turn things upside down once more." This comment is applicable to the interpretation of 16:25–33.

27. Bultmann, *John,* 591.

28. Duke (*Irony in the Fourth Gospel,* 57–58) notes that the superficial confession of these verses is a source of their irony.

29. John 16:31 is grammatically ambiguous: because it is not introduced by an interrogative pronoun or adverb, it is not clear whether the verse should be read as a statement or a question (BDF #440). The 26th edition of Nestle punctuates the sentence as a question, and that is the reading accepted by the majority of scholars.

30. Duke (*Irony,* 57 n. 36) notes that Jesus speaks ironically here and

thereby underscores the error of the disciples' perception that Jesus will no longer speak in a figure.

CONCLUSION

1. For a discussion of the use of the ascent/descent language to speak of Jesus' death in the Fourth Gospel, see Godfrey C. Nicholson, *Death as Departure. The Johannine Descent-Ascent Schema,* SBLDS 63 (Chico, Calif: Scholars Press, 1983).

2. See the definition of *hupsoō* in BAGD, 850. There is an interesting parallel to these two levels of meaning of *hupsoō* in the use of the Hebrew verb *nasa* in Genesis 40. Joseph's interpretation of the chief baker's dream hinges on the double meaning of *nasa* in Gen. 40:19: "Within three days Pharaoh will lift up your head—from you!—and hang you on a tree . . . ."

3. For treatments of the trial narrative that focus on the role of irony, see MacRae, "Theology and Irony," and Duke, *Irony in the Fourth Gospel,* 126–37. For the importance of this narrative for Johannine theology, see Josef Blank, "Die Verhandlung vor Pilatus. John 18.28—19.16 im Licht johanneischer Theologie," *BZ* 3 (1959):60–81.

4. For an interpretation of the trial before Pilate that is sensitive to the questions of power, authority, and truth, see Paul Lehmann, *The Transfiguration of Politics* (New York: Harper & Row, 1975), 48–70.

5. Amos N. Wilder, *Theopoetic: Theology and the Religious Imagination* (Philadelphia: Fortress Press, 1976), 92. See also Wilder's "The Word as Address and the Word as Meaning," in *The New Hermeneutic,* ed. James M. Robinson and John B. Cobb, Jr. (New York: Harper & Row, 1964), 198–218.

INDEX OF
BIBLICAL PASSAGES